Unless otherwise indicated, all Scripture quotations are taken from the Holy Bible, King James Version Scripture taken from the Holy Bible, New INTERNATIONAL VERSION AE. Copyright 1973, 1978, 1984 International Bible Society. All rights reserved throughout the world. Used by permission of International Bible Society.

PISS IN MY FACE AND TELL ME IT'S RAINING

ISBN 978-1-940831-02-2
Copyright © 2011 by Tina Perry

Published by Gifted Minds Publishing, LLC.
Email: info@giftedmindspublishing.com
Website: www.Tina M Perry.com

All rights reserved. Except as permitted under the United States Copyright Act of 1976, no part of this publication may be reproduced or distributed in any form or by any means, or stored in a data base or retrieval system, without the prior written permission of the publisher.

Printed in the United States of America

DEDICATION

I would like to dedicate my book to the Lord Jesus Christ. In loving memory of my parents, Skimmie and Syplina Perry. I love you, and I always cherish you and the time God gave us. Milah Perry, Auntie, misses and will always love you too. Dajun, my heart, son, rest in peace! To my brothers and sisters that have gone on before me: Charles, Kenneth, and Patricia, you are always in my heart. To my Sister Gwendolyn, you told me right before you passed that I had a gift called Poetic Justice; Do not to take it for granted but embrace it. Thank you, Sister, I love you and will always hold those words dear to my heart!

Dear Heavenly Father, I give you the honor, glory, and the praise. I pray that as these pages unfold, old things would pass away and behold that all things would become new, in the name of Jesus! I pray that you would release your healing balm over everyone, that's going through relationship issues. I pray for the ones in abusive relationships that you would set in their path a way of escape. I pray that the captive would be set free. I pray that every woman reading this book is endowed with discernment, that God would anoint our eyes to spot the enemy a mile away. I pray that minds would be stirred, healed, delivered, and restored, then, elevated. Father, I ask that you restore their faith. I pray in the name of Jesus that the person who is saying I cannot go any further, oh God, you would cover them with a sense of peace that the anointing released will let them know they can make it for there is hope in Christ Jesus. Father you said one will plant the seed, another will water it, and then you will bring the increase. Father, we bless you in advance for the increase.

I take authority over every spirit that would come to cause a distraction. I bind it and loose clarity of thought. I bind every mind binding demon; in the name of Jesus. In Jesus great name I pray, Amen!

ACKNOWLEDGMENTS

I would like to give thanks to God who is the Author and Finisher of my Faith. My Children: Carlos, I thank you for the unconditional love you have always given me I thank you for all your love and support! Diamond, you are the daughter that many people dream of having I truly Thank you for all you do. To my one son Mike Kelso, only God knows how much I love and appreciate you. Son, you jumped in and rolled your sleeves up took your time and got the job done! Tanino you are my little rock, always seeming to know when I'm weary, always saying, "Mom I got you." Crystal I didn't have you but you are mine. Thank you for all you do. Auntie loves you to pieces. I have to tell God thank you again because he has blessed me with the best children ever! Tia I thank you for seeing a need and stepping up your act of kindness was golden. I will never forget what you did for me. Derico, Ms. Cassidy, and Demir you bring laughter to my soul. To my Brothers: Larry words can't begin to express my Gratitude when it comes to you. Curtis, you are living proof that God is still performing miracles. Auntie Delphine, I don't know what I would do without you - Super Auntie! I Promise you are the best. Thank you Tujuna for being super encouraging. My sisters, Shonie and Shalonnia, I love you, ladies. Tonya, my sister that don't sugar coat anything, thank you for all the help you have given me over the years. Special Thanks to Casino for imparting so, much vast knowledge. Shout out to Lachristian Davidson for being there. Shout out to Barb a.k.a. "Lady BEA" for always pushing me. I would like to give special thanks to Mr. Al Hartman for all your support and most of all for believing in me. Shout out to my good friend M.B., love you to the moon and back. Thanks to all my friends and family.

INTRODUCTION

"Piss In My Face and Tell Me It's Raining" was created to illustrate how to pinpoint deceit and generate awareness. I guarantee you this book will cause you to evaluate your life in every area and redirect your thinking. It will also touch down on why many women have breakups just to end up with the same man in a different body. There are countless stories that different women and I have experienced with the hopes that after reading this you wouldn't have to deal with these experiences.

Table of Content

1. She was Vulnerable....8
2. Know Your Role and Your Position...22
3. What???.........27
4. You Have the Right to Remain Silent............29
5. Consumed..........32
6. Dating.............34
7. Playboys and Players...........45
8. Remain a Challenge.............52
9. I Mastered the Art............60
10. Don't You Dare Settle.......63
11. You Sure Know How to Pick Them.....75
12. Master Deceivers............78
13. Divide and Conquer......82
14. Now That's Presentation....87
15. Do You Know Who You Are?........91
16. What's the Catch?......93
17. He was Clueless.....99
18. You are Going to Deep...............100

19. Out of the frying pan into the fire........103
20. One Summer Night...105

Chapter 1

She was Vulnerable

There was a story of a beautiful woman named Karen. Karen found herself in an unhappy long-term commitment that was literally draining her emotionally. Karen began to soul search she felt the process was hard but it gave her courage and strength to walk away. Karen was vulnerable and her situation was painful. She felt it was a hard decision but she knew that divorce was necessary. Karen often found herself questioning. "Hey! Whatever happened to happily ever after?" Karen was a woman who believed in love, marriage and family. Divorce was something Karen thought she would never experience. Well I am sure you are wondering why Karen wanted a divorce considering she had been in a marriage for over twenty years.

During this period she experienced countless heartaches and disappointments enduring the ups and downs and the hard patches. One might ask, "Why she stuck around so long?" She stayed because she loved her husband besides trial and error is how couples; learn one another. Well after being together for so long; their life goals changed. Karen felt she had outgrown her situation. She found herself emotionally beaten and bruised. Karen felt they had good and bad times. However the bad outweighed the good. Once on a hot day, Karen took the time and prepared a nice hot meal. She cooked black-eyed peas, rice, chicken and some cornbread. She had a couple of friends over, one ate. Her friend's response was "This food is the bomb!" What happened next was humiliating! She called her husband home for dinner.

Ron came home took a couple of bites then said: "This is nasty!" He spits it out and threw the rest in the garbage. Ron then went to the kitchen and made a bologna sandwich. Karen's friend looked over at her and said "Girl don't say anything. Ask him if he is full? If he says he is not then ask him, would he like you to fix him another sandwich?" Do not give him the easy way out.""Don't get upset with him. Or your anger will just make it easy for him to leave." Karen thought "That's smart!" and asked Ron "Would you like another sandwich?" He responded by saying "You talk too much!" as he slammed the door and boldly walked out. Ron was a secular rapper that did a lot of traveling. One might even call him a man of the world. Karen felt it was pretty hard to deal with him. One Afternoon Ron came downstairs with his suitcase packed around four in the afternoon without a word he preceded to the front door.

As he was walking out, he looked back and said: "By the way, my plane leaves at six AM." She replied "But that's in the morning. Where are you going tonight? When will you be back?" Ron responded "I am a grown man. I was kind enough to tell you I am leaving now get you some business." Ron stayed away a long time without any communication. It was months later when Ron returned. He was always in and out. Karen was fed up. Ron sensed it and expressed to Karen that he was sorry and wanted to start over. She agreed everything appeared to be going fine. However, out of the blue, Ron woke up and decided. He would move all his clothes, to his mom's house. Although Karen told him this was disrespectful, he expected her to accept it.

Ron would leave home dressed one way then return home dressed differently. Karen let him know she was uncomfortable. He let her know he made his decision and it was final. How convenient! However, he tried to soften the blow by letting her know. "I'm not leaving you! This is the place where I lay my head." Karen knew this was something that was unacceptable. However, she wanted to preserve her marriage, so she accepted it. One day Ron had company. Now this wasn't unusual. Considering Ron was popular. He often had company at the house but this day was different. One of Ron acquaintances named Joe came by to take care of some business. However, business wasn't the only thing on his agenda. Joe began complimenting her and revealed he was interested. He started saying, things like "I think you are beautiful. You belong with me." He went on to say "Ron could never afford the life that I could give you." Karen replied, "That's not my boyfriend you're speaking on that's my husband, and if you keep saying these things to me I am going to tell." Joe's response was "So what, tell him it's worth it! I want you!" Karen felt she should do the honorable thing so, she told Ron all that was said. Her HUSBAND'S response was "You don't check the pimp you check the Whore!" In disbelief, she said "REALLY."
***

This scenario is a good illustration of; however, your partner treats you around people will determine how his friends and family will treat you. I will touch down on this further into the chapters. Divorce is a very hard place. It does not matter whether you are ready, or not divorce can be a very emotional situation.

When dealing with an issue of this great magnitude be sure that you have a strong support system. Like friends, family or you may even need to seek professional counsel. There have been many people who have gone through a divorce. Most people don't like to talk about it because they feel it's much too personal. Karen never imagined that divorce could be that draining. She would find herself constantly replaying different scenes from their marriage. She became stressed dealing with all those emotions. Having so many questions... "Will I be able to live alone after sharing my bed and my life with someone for so long?" Karen felt the thought she found most draining was "I thought my husband and I would have been together forever?"

I'm sure dealing with divorce there will be a lot of what ifs. There will even be times when you will even consider going back for fear of not wanting to be alone.

It takes time, to learn another man. Then you will have questions like can you trust him? Will he fight you? Will he touch your children? "Believe it!" You are going to find yourself feeling depressed and lonely. These things can cause you to find yourself in a compromising situation, no matter, how well you think you have it all together! Trust me you will find yourself going over things said and done in the relationships. You will entertain many thoughts and questions. **Karen said," The one question that stood out in my mind was why? Was I not good enough? Was there something I could have done to preserve my marriage?"** She felt she needed answers, but she knew she had to move on. But here is a clincher.

When trying to move on to your next relationship the first thing your new mate does, will cause emotions that are lying dormant to surface such as blame, hurt, anger, and trust issues. For example, you may feel if your ex-had respected, honored, and loved you, then you wouldn't have to deal with new hurt. But, here is a helpful nugget that may help. If you're mental capacity is strong enough to move forward, the one thing I found to be true is there is a difference between talking to and talking at one another. Once you learn the difference, you will discover that you are one step closer to understanding. However, if you can't move forward, then this would be an indication that you need closure. This part of the process is where you sit down and discuss what went wrong while remaining calm? If all goes well, it should lead to the next step HEALING. Did you know that healing is the process that makes you healthy again while discovering what tore your relationship apart? Here is the grand opportunity where you can ask questions you know the usual ones.

Why did it have to come to this? What was it I did wrong? Was it the way I carried myself? Was there another? Was there anything; I did not give you that you desired that would cause you not to be the man you could have been. Take responsibility for the things that you've done or should have done. By doing so, you and your partner can move forward. Please bring your honesty remember we have to be true to ourselves. If there are any questions you feel will be productive towards closure do not tiptoe around your issues. **Just ask**! You could receive some solid answers that will help you to obtain your healing. There will also be many uncertainties that arise.

You will find yourself in a position wondering about love such as why; did God allow me to go through this? Is there a thing called love? Is there hope? Oh yeah, there is hope. There are plenty of women that have overcome the bad and moved on to better relationships. Here is a tip! Allow God to fix you before you even entertain another relationship. Combine Gods principals with intellect when your next partner is picked. Then trust him in your process not only is he equipped to restore you but he will do it with compassion. He will even love you past all your hurts and insecurities being patient and understanding. Not quick to throw you away.

Not to mention, God will NOT put you in situations that could damage you more. Now Back to Karen….Karen said, "There wasn't any physical abuse However, there was definitely a lot of mental abuse." Mental abuse is **just** as bad as physical abuse. **Mental abuse:** consist of things being said or done example. You are too fat and nobody wants you. You're ugly and you need to comb your hair. Take notes from some of these other women and learn how to put your clothes together; you look a mess. Then when he knows he has your attention. He will end it with don't you realize I am doing you a favor by being with you? I could have been with someone far prettier. **Oh yes mental abuse is real!** I believe this next story is a good illustration. Why some women go to prison.

***

  Mona was dating Stan. They were in engage with the promise of a ring. Not only was her love for him above the clouds but it had past the moon. Mona would have told you she had a picture perfect relationship with four beautiful children. (Mona was blinded by love).

One afternoon a friend of Mona's named Tish called to ask why she did not tell her Stan had gotten married. Mona replied, "He did not get married, GIRL! Do not listen to gossip. He and I have plans this evening." So, Tish began to explain how she seen his family coming from somewhere all dressed up. How she'd asked a neighbor what was going on? They replied, "Stan got married," Tish confused replied "Ohhhh they got married!" Wondering why Mona did not invite her they explained, "No! Stan married someone else." (At this point, the light switch in her brain turned on). Mona became furious by this information she began thinking how could this happen. So Mona didn't call Stan she just kept busy until it was time for her date. While Stan was still at the room he told Ce-Ce his now new wife he had to go tie up his loose ends then he headed to Mona, for their dinner date.

Mona didn't let him know that she even had a clue. Mona and Stan were sitting having small talk. When Mona questioned, "Do you have anything you would like to share with me?" He replied, "What that I love you! He then looked her in her eyes and said "You know you are the only girl for me." Stan smiled at Mona as he pulled her in his arms saying, "But you know that already!"They continued with dinner Mona found her self-growing angrier and quite agitated. This situation was not sitting well with her he could clearly tell something was bothering Mona. He began to feel guilty. So he came clean and told her not only did he get married to Ce-Ce but she came into their marriage with six kids. He then revealed he met her on a business trip! He said, "It started as nothing but they soon fell in love." He began to explain how he never meant to hurt her he told her, "He loved her and his biological children." You see he loved Mona but he was not in love with her.

Stan felt that he and Mona had a good thing. Stan told Mona, "Look if it's not broke why fix it." Mona was outraged, by his words yet she remained a lady in public. However, no matter how hard she tried she could not hold back her tears. They continued their conversation after dinner and returned back to her place, where things became heated and confrontational. Mona began to scream, "I hate you! How dare you, take on six children that are not yours.
"You say you can barely take care of our four." He replied, "Look my love for you didn't change so, our relationship shouldn't either." Mona said, "In that moment everything faded to black." Mona became more enraged she began Screaming and fighting him, not only was she hurt, but she was deeply embarrassed everyone knew but her! At this point he did not want to let Mona go they had been together, for so long he felt that they should continue.

Remember in the earlier part of this story I spoke about engagement. It is very clear that she was the only one engaged. Men sometimes play on our emotions with words and mind games that lead to situations like this. Stan expects Mona to become his mistress. Mona felt she should have been Stan's wife Mona said, "I felt destroyed with constant thoughts of Stan now belonging to another woman." She said, "I felt myself trembling in agonizing pain. Thinking I had him first." Mona said, "She fell to the floor screaming! "Ohhhh God! What I am going to do? I want to kill him." Stan watched Mona go through every emotion and every hurt. But it still wasn't enough to make him stay. Mona said, "If it had not been for my children I would have killed him." This is how many women end up in prison. Mona gave her everything to a man that didn't consider her or his children priority.

I have to Say this has to be one of the worst things that could happen to a woman in love. Question, does this make him a bad man or could this reflect he was just the wrong man for Mona? I think in a situation like this its best to gather what's left of your dignity and move on. Just think! You got in your car and started moving forward. In that split second you decided. *I think I want to go backwards.* So you throw your car in reverse while looking over your shoulder and accelerate. However, in that split second. You become tired of looking over your shoulder so you face forward without taking the car out of reverse. What do you think will be the outcome? Someone could get hurt your assets could be damaged and lives could be destroyed. The same thing holds true for life you have to decide not to look back. You have to move forward with your life and allow yourself to move forward.

Program it in your mind I'm not looking back. This step will produce a positive change take a chance! Move forward! Don't sit around rehearsing or nursing your past release your fear and step out. Once you have achieved this mindset. Congratulations are in order you have taken your first step forward. Next, take time to build your strength. Remove all the clutter get on the road, and head to a positive direction. Listen God's word assured us if we do not give up! Love will be good to us if we wait. God's word teaches us. Hold fast to your confession of faith. Remember! Good things come to those, who wait. Trust God! We have to know that it is in God's timing things are accomplished while dealing with life issues. We have to learn to be patient. You must disconnect yourself from your past in order to deal with your now, keep moving; never allowing yourself to become stagnate. Accessing everything, God has in store for your future! Now back to Karen...

Divorce was Karen's last option but she knew she could not remain in a relationship where she felt like she was slowly dying emotionally. One morning Karen woke up it became crystal clear. This was her moment of truth a decision had to be made stay or move forward? Karen decided to move forward and begin divorce procedures. This was painful yet necessary. However, somehow Karen always managed to produce a smile. On the outside Karen looked like a masterpiece but, on the inside she was broken. In this season Karen had to learn to trust God for every decision she made. Karen continued to pray and knew in her heart this was the right decision. One day she woke up and realized that they had grown apart. Karen had once been eager to do anything Ron, asked her to make him happy. No matter how unhappy it made her even if she felt conflicted about it; she still did it. Karen tried for years to make it work one day it came to a point where Karen no longer cared. Karen prayed for, her marriage for countless years. However, you should know something God is not a man that he should lie nor, son of man that he should repent!

Numbers 23:19
God is not a man, that he **should lie**; neither the son of man, that he **should** repent: hath he said, and shall he not do it? Or hath he spoken, and shall he not make it good?

Everything that God spoke concerning their marriage came to past. Ron did realize that he loved his wife. Ron also came to the realization. That Karen was the best thing for him. In the beginning, Ron gave Karen a hard time about going to church Ron knew in his heart he couldn't lose Karen. However, he is now ready to do anything including church.

He began to say, "I will go! I will do anything to save my marriage." Sad to say, by this time Karen was done. However, in Ron's mind divorce was out of the question. They had separated many times but, every time they parted Karen found herself broken, and her self-esteem shattered. Karen kept finding herself right back in the same situation. Feeling stupid subjected to the same emotional abuse. Then she would run to the alter crying out open before God seeking deliverance and restoration. However, this time it was different she had been fasting and praying. So, she felt there was no need for deliverance. Karen thought she had it all together she was very wrong deliverance was just what she needed. Not getting delivered became one of the worst decisions Karen ever made. Every time Karen decided to move on, Ron would be sent back by the enemy (The devil) leaving her emotionally distraught and tore down. Although, this time Karen could see a difference and recognized true sincerity, she could see Ron was ready for real commitment.

However, she was ready for change Ron had finally taken her to a place of no return. Then unexpectedly a man from her past appeared. During this time, the divorce was becoming final. Karen had been with her husband for twenty- four years. Karen began to experience the different emotions that were taking place and stated that the divorce began to feel like a process. Karen knew at this point it was not going to be easy. After much emotional turmoil the divorce was final. Ron needed closure, so he questioned. "You've been taking my stuff for so long. What happen to make you change and stop taking it now?" She thought, "That's easy" then Karen replied, "Have you looked at me I do not have too!"

Divorce can land you into some crazy predicaments like the story that's about to unfold. **During this time Karen began seeing Tim, he began to make her feel that maybe not all hope was gone. He told her he just needed one woman in his life. What Karen should have done next was to investigate his motives and who sent him was it God or the devil? Ladies, she did a no-no.** She shared her pass abuse how she gave Ron her best and how Ron had taken her for granted not knowing in the end. Tim would use everything against her. He began Showering Karen with words of encouragement and adoration he would say you're so beautiful, where I go you too should be there too. Tim spent time with her every night he made her feel that he too had been the victim.

He shared countless intimate stories to show he had been hurt. Tim began to tell her REASSURE her that she could trust him. Tim would say, "I know the last man hurt you but I am a loving man, sensitive to your needs. If you were to fall, I would catch you just open up and let me in." She began to spend every moment she could with Tim. He appeared to be a genuine man like a (Fairy tale in the making). He was someone who expressed his emotions it was as though he wore his emotions on his sleeves. **Karen thought is this the man! I have been waiting on all my life?"** Our mothers have always warned us not to deal with "GANGSTER" type men. We were taught they are dangerous but we were never warned, about the GAMESTER. A gamester is a brother who is a gambler. He prides himself on being; slicker than oil he's someone who is charming and smooth with his words. He will smile and speak elegant words. A gamester feels if he articulates his words, well enough he can sell you a bridge.

He will fabricate a story that would appear so; real it would almost have him believing it. A gamester's ploy is to run circles around you. I can recall as a child witnessing Jay and Denise's marriage. Jay became bored so, he decided to have an extra marital affair? He packed his bags and moved in with Rita. Rita was Jay's new girlfriend/babysitter. On the weekends, he would get his children. Although if Denise called him stating she needed a break or a little TLC (tender, love, and care). He would go pick his children up and drop them off to Rita, and she would bathe and comb their hair making sure all their needs were met. Rita would do anything to win Jay's affections. Jay was dark skin with pearly white teeth he was charming, handsome and debonair. Jay had a way with the ladies he would make love to Rita take her shopping then he would return home to his wife and spend romantic weekends. One evening Rita had a funny feeling so, she put the kids in the car and went to Denise's house. It was said when Rita got there Jay and Denise were sitting on the porch kissing and playing around, Denise was sitting on jays lap.

Rita jumped out the car screaming! "What's going on?" That's when Denise stood up and asked, "What are you doing here?" Denise then proceeded to Rita's car kissed and hugged her children at this point, Jay stood up and said, "Listen don't make a scene on me and my wife." Get in the car take my kids home I'll be there in a little while. It was said Rita walked back to the car and shouted, "I'm not gone keep being your fool and pulled off." Jay put his arm back around Denise and they continued; enjoying their evening. Yes Rita was angry but she didn't want to lose Jay's love. It would appear that Denise actually had the upper hand. Sad to say neither of the two were winners. In all actuality, No woman is willing to share her husband.

I hear women say all the time **I know I am not number two.** My response when I hear this is, "You shouldn't want to be number one." They generally have a look of confusion. My reasoning for this is I can't be his number one or his number two. I have to be the ONLY one. Now let's get back to the story!

Once while in the bathroom. Tim was shaving he made a comment. He said, "Karen should buy her son some clippers. He said "The one thing her son should not do is stand directly in front of the mirror he should stand back. If you stand off and look you will see the hairline much clearer. I took this illustration and equated it to relationships. You see sometimes your mate plays games but you're so blinded by love you cannot see all the issue and things at hand. So sometimes it's good to step back take a little time and evaluate your situation not only will you be able to see everything around you but you will be able to see everything much clearer!

Chapter 2

Know Your Role and Your Position

Karen was a woman with strong compassion. She believed Tim and began to let her guard down. Alert: she really thought she had it all together. She had been fasting for almost a year. Up every night at two am until six am, for months praying and crying out to God. Karen had a very strong fast and prayer life. However, somehow she still ended up falling from grace.

Passage <u>Luke 4</u> : [1]And Jesus being full of the Holy Ghost returned from Jordan, and was led by the Spirit into the wilderness, [2]Being forty days tempted of the devil.

The chemistry was through the roof there was a divine connection, or so she thought. Karen would have never thought Tim learning her was not for the purpose, to strengthen her. NEVER did she think he could have been studying her to, use all that he had learned to tear her down! Tim even told her he LOVED her. What did she do to him? She didn't fall for Tim because of the money he could offer or, for the way he could make her feel in the bedroom. Tim captured her by the way he showered her with love. He was making love to her mind, Karen MISSED companionship and love. However, the intimacy did play a big part. Karen and Tim had a big blow out afterwards they had an intimate moment. Tim asked her, "Is this! What you wanted?" It is amazing how some men think they have the keys. These keys consist of spending time with us getting us in the bedroom and sexing us then take us out to wine and dine us. Oh yeah! Give us some money to do a little shopping will makes things all better. The only thing this does is pacify us for the moment.

There are several types of pacifiers. This was an illustration of one. This is not good for the relationship the next issue experienced will cause the woman to explode. This is why it is important to resolve issues. But some men don't think they have to fix the mess, they have created and they try to avoid resolving the issues, as if the problem will magically disappear. When men know they are wrong or have done something wrong. They feel they need to cover the cut with a bandage but what they really have to do is heal the wound. When you deeply cut yourself and go the hospital. The first thing the Doctor is going to do is! Access the situation and examine the wound at that point he is going to give you some sort of pain killer. Clean the wound with some kind of antiseptic to keep the infection, from entering and spreading. Next, he is going stitch you up. Then advise you to cover the stitches; to protect the wound. He will then instruct you to remove the bandage in a few days. So the air can assist with the healing process. Doctors will usually use the dissolvable stitches or, the ones you have to come back and have removed.

Reason being, sometimes after you remove the stitches the wound is still open. In the event this happens you may require a little more attention. This is why Doctors are in place and healing is necessary. When a man gets caught the first thing they need to do is access the situation to see how much damage has been done. He needs to do everything in his power to ease the pain and comfort you. He needs to clean up his mess and give you some air so, healing can begin he should separate from any situation. That could contaminate you. He needs to take whatever measure needed to stitch your relationship back together. After being addressed some situations' just work out. While some wounds/ situations still need care. At this point, he needs to be very considerate of your feelings.

He also needs to lay everything out and tell the truth. I need you to pay attention! Here is a vital point if he insists on lying and his actions don't change he's not sorry nor, is ready to move forward and fix things. What he is telling you is that he is not sincere, and he is **still** going to play. You see men and women are so different. When it comes to being faithful in relationship here is where a lot of the trouble comes in. A woman will come across a man's path and because most men are visual, he will see a woman and **not think, he will usually react**. Most women **think** and, we feel. A woman will see a man and, think goodness he is so fine, and then we will say in our heart I love Billy boy I can't do that to him. I said most **women**...Now back to my point. **If** a man thinks the relationship is worth salvaging. He's going to think things through. There is one thing for certain; two things for sure, if he is man enough, he's going to find a way for the two of you to come together so, he can take accountability for his actions correct the problem and figure out why it happened. Usually, when most men, get caught they down play how we feel. Some are sensitive and some are unsympathetic, when it comes to how they handle our feelings. We as women have to come with a better mind set our feelings are important too.

We have to stop being so, accepting to whatever is offered to us. As women we need to raise, the standards. **We need more! Let's get back to the story. ***Karen was actually amazed Tim even thought like that. The truth was all she wanted was to love Tim. Karen began to observe how he threw caution to the wind. Tim had two or three women he dealt with in the same capacity (No protection). This brother was so, confident and creative he felt he would never get caught up never stopping to think that one of the other women could catch on to his game.**

In return she starts seeing someone else with the mindset tonight may not be my turn with Tim therefore, it is not Tim's turn with me tomorrow, and she sleeps with someone else and the condom breaks! That's if she even bothers to use one. Now, what if tragedy strikes and she becomes infected? The next time she's with Tim she will make love to him as usual (No protection) without a second thought about oh how this could affect everyone in this circle of deceit; everyone's life would be in danger. It is very clear that Tim deceived Karen to keep her. He made Karen feel as though she was the only one. Why couldn't he give her, the benefit of the doubt? By saying, "He didn't want a committed relationship." Instead he set her up for failure. Why couldn't Tim just be honest?

Karen had been honest with him! When dealing in situations it is always good to know your roll. (Know exactly where you stand). Know your position; are you important in his life? Are you just friends? If so, what kind of friends are you? This will help you to maneuver keeping you covered in a safe place. {This means having the ability to protect your heart}. **It is so, crazy because Karen was so, insecure but she had never been or, felt so sure. She is now sensing a change in Tim's behavior. There has been a shifting in their relationship. She's begun questioning what's wrong! Did something happen? Tim lets her know I feel you are too friendly. Karen begins to start handling things differently anything she felt that would make him uncomfortable she just wouldn't do. Karen began to disconnect herself from males she knew were interested in her. Not only did Karen care for Tim she cared how her actions affected him. Isn't life funny?** Early on in the chapters I spoke about how men do things to pacify women.

I just want to expound on this just for a minute. There are a lot of women rocking engagement rings. Now, let me say this, there is nothing wrong with being engaged. I think it's a beautiful thing to be engaged. But ladies how long do you have to wait on the promise? I have heard men say they only gave their girl a ring; **just** to shut her up. So, if you are engaged over a year or two, what are you waiting on? Has there been a date set? Has the dress been picked and being paid on? Are you saving for a big extravagant wedding and honeymoon? Question, you do know big weddings are for the guest's entertainment right? The day of your wedding, it is important that the minister you and the one you love are present, anything else is optional.

Now if you're the type that must have the big lavish wedding then by all means go for it. This will also break down every excuse cutting down on time and eliminating stress. I need you to reevaluate these things. Now, let me ask you have you been giving a ring or, a pacifier? Never allow a man to put a limit on your worth. Your mate should always exhibit how important you are in his life. I decided a long time ago the next man I allow in my life, will have to love me like I am the only woman in the world. I refuse to be treated with nothing less; than the utmost respect.

Chapter 3

What???

How many know that rain is good for growth but we must be careful of all impostors! Just because it comes showering down. Please don't automatically assume its rain, sometimes things just are not what they seem. My mother once told me, "Baby people will piss in your face and tell you it's raining." I never understood what she meant until I started dating. Ladies I encountered a brother that felt, I should understand when he would disappear for a few days and not answer his phone. When questioned he would say, "I didn't trust him and I doubted his love." That's when I had my Ah Ha moment. I said, "Oh!!!!! This is what she was talking about." Sometimes men enter in our lives. The first thing we think is! Is this it? We have to learn to stop being so, free with our emotions.

We have to be careful not to be anxious, and so, giving of ourselves. We need to learn to be patient and watch. Here is a key study his behavior and listen get this if you listen to a person long enough they will tell you exactly who they are and where they are coming from. **Karen started to notice the showers she was use to were turning into something else. It went from the introduction of this is my future wife, to being introduces as this is my friend. One day they were at one of his family member's home. While they were there he began introducing or shall I say REDUCING her to the title friend. She was hurt! Tim led her to believe that he was the missing link to her future. He began trying to alter her thinking. However, it was set in her mind I will always speak what's on my mind without being intimidated.**

Ladies learn the signs so; it won't be hard to recognize the real deal. Now let us look at this why would a man that loves a woman jump through hoops to make a connection then later disrespect her. It's simple he doesn't love her he just wanted sex. The truth of the matter is a man will do everything in his powers to restore you.

***One of my family members named Cookie was dating a guy who was a cheat; her boy friend and my boy friend at the time were best friends. One day I came home from shopping and Cookie's boyfriend was sitting in my house with another female. I immediately said, "If you don't get her out of here... I don't play that!" So, they left and the new girl he was seeing had her hair styled in a bob. Later her boyfriend went home and told Cookie, "I saw a nice hairstyle that would look nice on you!" The next day Cookie got up, went to the beauty shop and had her hair styled in a bob. When I saw her, I could not believe my eyes! I said, "Cookie what made you go get your hair styled like that?" She said, "Her man had requested her to do so." Cookie has always been the kind of girl that accommodated her man. A few days later Cookie had some down time so she decided to surprise her boyfriend with lunch. Cookie said, "When I pulled in the parking lot there was my boyfriend hugged up with his other girlfriend." Cookie jumped out her car and exploded. The young lady ran screaming into her job. Cookie said, "I fought my boyfriend with everything I had." If you are wondering, he got fired and Cookie went to jail. Cookie found out the hard way that experience is a teacher. Cookie's incarceration taught her not to be so accommodating after her stay in jail.

Chapter 4

You Have the Right to Remain Silent

There is something I must touchdown on we as women make this crucial mistake. We meet a man and tell him all about our past. For, instance my ex stayed out all night or, he was a cheater. When I was a child someone raped me. My last boyfriend beat me or, you may have told them I did not complete high school big mistake! The first time you have an altercation he will take what you said and use it against you. We have to start letting men figure us out. I say, we should be a little bit more mysterious. Have you ever met a guy and he only said just enough to make you want to know more about him? I think when it's done by a woman being gracefully and mysterious, can be very attractive. It keeps men guessing and wanting more.

While having conversation give out less information listen and try to gather all the information you can, like what condition are they in concerning their physical and mental health? What's his credit score can he hold down a job? Is he a drinker? How often? What does he do for recreation? Find out what his temper is like is he disrespectful and will he fight a woman? Here is an exp: Why you never divulge everything about your past. If your last boyfriend beat you and you told the new boyfriend. That very man will say I would never hit you but take on a very different stance if an argument arose. He would become angry and would be quick to strike you. Now if he's not a woman abuser he will state this is why your last guy hit you. Why, you have given him ammunition against you. Here is another example. If you expressed that your last man wasn't affectionate. Your new guy would be sure to kiss and make love to you every time he laid eyes on you.

Most men will take the time to study you to see what it is that makes you tick. Learning what he needs to work on making sure he gets everything, down to a science. He will begin to mend your broken heart by comforting you spending time and listening to you. He will become very attentive to your every need. For, instance if you want a foot rub he will be more than happy to accommodate you. Now after he feels like he's secured you. He will begin breaking you down. He will start telling you things like. "You act like you don't recognize how good I am to you. Don't you understand that my time is of the essence? Yet! I'm spending it with you." He will get angry at every small thing; you say or do. Threatening to end the relationship!

He will say, "If you don't want this relationship to be over then you will comply with my rules." Always look for flags, and **never** ignore them. You should start becoming very alert. If he openly tells you I do not want to make a commitment. This would mean you are not the only one. He will question, "Do you want to keep receiving this good loving? If so then get your stuff together and be a good girl, get in line and except it." Why, he has studied you he knows you are going to crave his love and attention. He's very aware that he's in control of your emotions. He's calculated how to push every button. If his accuracy is correct he can successfully complete the equation. He will take all your hurts wounds and bruise and nurse you back. Just so, he can **BREAK** you the goal is to manipulate and control you. **Karen soon started to question Tim**

"What is this I am seeing?" She asked, "If you and I are in a relationship why are you yet, dealing with other women? How are your other friendships at the same level as ours, why are other women calling and questioning you better yet, why are you explaining? When baby all you need is right here?"

Tim quickly replied and tried to shift the blame on her. At this point Karen is in a difficult place her heart is exposed! She could never hurt him. Tim began to tell her "Baby, I am not pissing on you, what is happening is normal. You're tripping. It's raining!" Karen replied, "But baby, this can't be rain its yellow and it smells like ammonia. BOY the rain that falls from the sky has a fresh scent."Tim then said, "See you're looking at things from the wrong angle. See baby, it's only yellow because the sun is shining the rain just looks yellow, that's all baby!" Karen then replies, "But baby this is sticky." He responds, "That's because the sun is so hot not only are you delusional the heat is causing you to think things are there, that are not which causes you to work yourself up. That is just your sweat baby I can assure you that its rain and not piss."

***This was an illustration of how a man will do you wrong. You may even catch him red-handed and he will still try to make you think you're crazy! *** Sade and Trent had been dating for about a year. Sade worked the midnight shift she became ill on the job so she got off work and went home. When she turned the key she went in and didn't turn any lights on she just undressed and climbed in bed, that's when she felt something wet and then she felt a woman's breast. She said, "I immediately started cursing and swinging we began to rumble when I heard the unidentified woman's voice. I quickly ran to turn the light on, and to my amazement it was my cousin. So I ran to the kitchen and grabbed a butcher knife. Sade said,

"My boyfriend and my cousin both quickly ran out the front door naked." Unbelievable!!!

Chapter 5

Consumed

A Man/woman not grounded is not safe they are like a live wire on the ground. Be careful not to tamper with someone who is a live wire not to step on him or her. (WARNING)Someone could become emotionally or, physically hurt leaving them scarred for life. In some cases the results could be something more tragic. DEATH! Oh yes they will kill you. This is where we as women should come in and ground that wire out. When grounding out the negative wire you will need love and compassion. You will also need the ultimate source; which is God. Women are born nurtures by nature. Some women are also born natural homemakers. My point is if you want to consider yourself wife material we must be willing to turn a house into a home, while learning how to help him follow his dreams and build his ambitions.

Always assuring him he can reach the stars. You have to become a praying woman willing to seek God read your word and fast. You have to be willing to utilize these key things until, they no longer have the desire to run wild or, acquire the ability to settle. Studies show that drug and alcohol use in the homes cause a high percentage of abuse in homes. Some men/women become influenced by a source of power that has a negative driving force not being able to control their emotions. Beware these are the components of a live wire.

Another source would be bad experiences in prior relationships. ***

Things were happening so, fast Karen did not know what was happening. She felt such a connection she began to smile again. She would wake up in the morning her first thought would be Tim! He would also be her final thought for, days she walked around in a daze. Then Karen found herself bumping into things. Then out of nowhere Karen had an eye opening experience. She began to see herself falling so, she yells to him HELP! She is now plunging to the ground; at an unknown magnitude. Karen is very afraid and her heart is pounding at unknown rate. She is screaming for, Tim he has become so, consumed he can't hear her. Tim has become so, disconnected that he cannot see her in distress. However, what he does see is a woman over reacting. In Tim's mind he has everything under control. Tim does not feel a need to respond to the situation. Tim is not taking any action to catch nor rescue Karen!

Nevertheless, he tells Karen to relax!

I got you just go with the flow!

Trust me everything is ok baby!

There is one thing ladies. **Men can only do, what we allow them too.** Case and Point! My friend's husband stayed out all night in anger she began questioning him, "Where have you been? Who were you with? He responded, "Shut up." With a look of confusion she responded, "Huh!" " You don't tell me to shut up." He replied, "Oh you disrespect me now?" He began choking her and threw her against the wall after she stopped coughing and caught her breath. She said, "I told him, to get his things and get out." He responded, "I am sorry baby I was just trying to see how far I could go.

Chapter 6

Dating

The rules of the dating have certainly changed. Men use to court women now people meet and have sex on the same day. ~ FYI~ when a man meets a woman he will let her know that he does not want her to change. The two main things are usually weight and personality. Ladies here is another nugget you can't stop doing the things you did to get him. However, nine times out of ten we do change. Why, because men put on facade to attract women selling us Dreams and Promises. Most women often come off as angels when they first start dating; later the men get met with attitude. Why, because most times people don't introduce you to the person they really are, they send their representative.

Case and scenario: He will put on airs just to capture you. Here is something else you can bet your bottom dollar on. He's going to get tired of pretending just pay attention. While having conversations, I've heard several females say they felt they have met men and it appeared as if they were their knight in shining armor. They wanted to be super excited but, past relationships prevented them; from enjoying it. Take the time to listen and pay attention. Who they are will be revealed. I guarantee you if their intentions are not pure they will drop the ball. Here is a sure fire sign to look for they will start fabricating and their true colors; will come out. Now, if what he is saying is true and he is truly trust worthy. The results of the relationship could be a lot different. Here's a twist to why they drop the ball. Sometimes, men aren't fabricating they have intentions, on doing the right thing.

However, what the women had to offer wasn't enough for them to want to take it; to the next level. Let me explain, not having enough clear gathered information will stir his mind up and cause him to have questions. Will she hold a job? Will she help with the bills and clean up? Will I get good home cooked meals? Will this one truly love me? Can she truly be faithful to one man? If he thinks he's ready for someone new. He will think... I know my present relationship is not working. But I have been with her forever should I leave my girl for her? Would leaving my current situation be a bad move? Will I place myself in a worst position, could she argue more than the one I am with? Can I trust her? Sometimes they become scared with draw and drop the ball. Because the fear of the unknown. Allow me to take a minute and examine new dating ethics. I know it is a new day and age; for dating. The rules have definitely changed women now days have men screwed up. The men think the women are the providers. We need to get back to the basics not only to reflect the softer side of a woman but to reestablish respect and bringing back chivalry.

What happened to men opening up your car door or, just opening the door period? My belief is men should send flowers not because they are in the doghouse but just because! A man should recognize when a woman steps in his **presence that he has been gifted with a present**. The man in your life should realize you are a gift and that your presence is a present. He should immediately greet you take your coat. He should hold your hand, pull your chair out before you sit when it's time to leave, your date should be ready to assist you with your coat and when you get to the car open your car door. A man dating you should go out of his way to make you feel special. These are small gesture but they go along way.

There are a few more things concerning chivalry but, I will touch down on them later. Here are some first date rules. First, date find an event outdoors some where you both can be comfortable. There is no reason why he can't take you out to a dinner or a show? The only reason a man usually shows resistance is, he doesn't want to be seen with you in public or, it is a strong probability you don't holds his interest. Then you, should have a problem if the only date, he wants to offer is an evening of sexual activities at his home; watching TV and listening to music. This should be a deal breaker. I have a friend that says when she goes on a date with a guy. If he does not, open her car door. He will not get another date. His actions will cause him to be an immediate turn off. Ladies please believe me when I tell you men love a challenge and a woman that respects herself. Here is a question that I must pose. What happened to purity? I found that a female that has not been with a man (A virgin) could be likened as a Goddess

She is the girl who would not allow her temple to be defiled. She is the girl desired by every man but no one can have. Think about it! What measures do you think men will take? For a woman that holds on to her goods. He will give her everything she wants. Why, because of her stance {which is I'm saving myself for marriage}. She has learned to stay out of tempting situations. Not only does she hold the keys to the world. She's well aware that she has the upper hand. Now a day's people just want relations (sex). They are not looking for relationships. The same way most people treat God. Everybody now days will tell you I am hooked up with God. "I'm saved!" Just without the sacrifices and commitment.

Women use to have morals and guidelines which consisted of men having to wait. Today I do not know what's going on! People meet at the bus stop and have sex right there. One thing, I can certainly say is; I was not ready for the dating game.

*** I was speaking with a young woman named Sam who said, "I had a bad experience, with a particular man that I had been dating." She said, "I thought we had a connection he treated me like a queen until one evening we were sitting around smoking marijuana." She said, "He got up and left the room for a few minutes. When he came back he had a strange look on his face. It was like he was a different person Sam furthered, "He started to make his move on me. I did everything I could to stop him. However, I was not strong enough.

The more I said "No "The more he became aggressive. He ripped my shirt open and tore my bra off, as he began reaching for my pants. He stopped and looked me in my eyes, bald his fist up; and said, "Stop playing with me." This is what we call date rape. Sam said my friend began to say, "You are a grown woman, I thought you knew what you wanted." she said, "I began to cry" he told her, "You make me sick." I never want to see you again" She then said, "I felt bullied, betrayed, and hurt. She never saw or heard from him again." But listen what she should have done was report him to the police, and had him arrested and prosecuted. **No** means NO! Please never allow anyone make you feel afraid or bad about saying No. Remember you have the right to say NO. In taking time and doing the research to write this book. I think what stood out to me the most was I found whether it was male or female.

There weren't too many people that didn't have a problem not wearing condoms, they appeared to be very nonchalant about who they slept with. What we as women need to understand is that men have sex to release and deposit. Women have sex to connect with the hope to create love and build long term commitment. Men impart we receive their seeds, and then we become the carrier of the baby the spirits or the STD's. You see these are totally different agendas. The bible states that when we have sex that we become one. This is the reason marriage is advocated. It is said when a man enters into a woman it creates a connection that binds you together in the spiritual realm. Sex is much **more than a just a good feeling it is the creation of soul ties. "A soul tie is the joining of two souls together like a bridge connecting one soul to another that could cause a positive or, a very negative effect. Let's look at the positive effects. Marriage will cause you to become one as it was intended.**

Matthew19:5 For this cause shall a man leave father and mother, and shall cleave to his wife: and they twain shall be one flesh."

Have you ever had a relationship? You thought you had moved on from but found yourself thinking. Why I am still strongly attached to that person not understanding why, you couldn't get over that person. The reason is because your souls have tied.

This is also is a way for demonic entry creating an opportunity, to use soul ties as a bridge to transfer spirits back and forth. This is how an opening can occur, and become very dangerous. This would be considered the negative side to soul ties. We have all have known someone that every time they opened their mouth they spoke a lie.

Well if you were to ever engage in sex, becoming one with them, it would not be strange if you got up and start fabricating. Soul ties are real and after a break, it is imperative that we ask God to break the soul ties. This goes to show you, we would avoid a lot of hassles not having sex before marriage. The average man usually can't wait for marriage to engage in sex. However, if you want to know it he if is tuned into God, this process will definitely determine what kind of man you are dealing with, it will separate the wheat from the tare. The other problem is that most, women can't wait for God to produce the man he has purposed for us or, clean up the one they have already. We are so; anxious we mess up everything then get upset, when we think God is not moving fast enough. We get so; excited about meeting a man and we can't wait to get to know him.

In the beginning we are on the phone almost every free moment we get. {Note} This is a crucial point believe it! He's open and you have his undivided attention. This is when you find out what he's made of women we really need to have some extended conversations. They call this part learning your man. I have this policy I do not tell men where I live I just keep putting them off or, I tell them my address right now is not important. If you take heed to this small piece of information it might save your life. I met several men and after a few conversations felt they weren't a good fit. When I would say I'm sorry but I am not comfortable with this the men would get so, angry and act crazy just imagine if they had of known where I resided, I more than likely would have had a few stalkers. Here is something else that is very important pay attention to the way, you communicate things. This will help set a standard for fine tooth communication. As I touched on earlier delivery and presentation is key for instance he might be one that cannot deal with criticism.

So, if you have a problem you will have to find a way to tell him without bringing him down. This will make things a lot smoother. It is important, that men don't see that they have the upper hand. It appears that they seem to respond better when they feel like they're losing their grip. In situations, like this is very important to remain calm not letting their actions bother you. You always want to be a part of the solution and never the problem. I was always taught one way to get your man to do something is, just to throw it out to him subtlety allowing room for, him to come back later, as if it were his idea. Instead of you saying, "That is what I told you!" Just act amazed Say, "Babe that is brilliant YES you should do that!" It is also, imperative that we must ask questions then wait to hear their response. We have to find a way to deal with men especially if you feel he's the one, be prepared when questioning a man, because more than likely he's going to answer it and respond with the same question. Please do not respond with, "I do not know" Be prepared to let him know exactly, what you want.

Also before, we get too involved with a man we should ask questions like have you ever been to prison? Have you ever been in a mental ward? Were your parents ever in one? What do you like to do? What movies do you like action, comedy or suspense? What is your favorite food? Do you drink or indulge in drugs? If not have you ever? Do you have children? Very important! If the answer is yes the next question should be "How many children do you have? Also do they share the same mother?" Be prepared if the answer is no, to deal with the drama and the different personalities that comes with it. Here is another question that no one likes to ask have you been tested for HIV? Another important question to ask is what is his full name but, don't stop there, ask to see his ID.

Let me tell you why, men have incorporated a few techniques, they use to set up their web of deceit. The first, part of the technique is giving out fake names. The second, one is having more than one cell phone, they have a cell phone for the woman wearing their ring and then they have a phone for their flings. The last part of this deceit is when they're done with you they don't just disregard the phones they disregard you too. The old saying says, "When you know better you do better." Situations like these occur so don't you dare think it's something wrong with you or that you're the only one. However, it is not personal it is just how this kind of man operates. **"Don't be their statistic!"** Once they have had their way with you. (Sex) Do not make it easy for them to say, "She was nothing." Making it is easier for them to move on.

We need to stay on top of things; the plan is to give them a run for their money. Ladies phone technology is growing at a fast rate. Educate yourself on the type of cell phone he has this is not for you to go through his phone. This is just to let him know you are not getting by with anything. You're probably wondering what I mean well let me tell you. The phone applications are incredible. Men can set it up to when their little jump offs calls (someone they keep around just for sex) their calls/text will be routed to another app in his phone. Appearing as though, the phone never ranged to make you look crazy. Oh I almost forgot ladies let's not forget about the video app that everyone is using. They record and communicate through video but here is the catch; it erases after so long. Also for my sisters that like to sneak through their man's phone beware they have a new app as soon as you press the wrong button it takes your picture. But here is the deal if you feel you have to go through his phone you don't trust him meaning you need to move on.

They also have an application they can type your number in and receive every text and every call **YOU** receive. Back to the subject! What is this new thing, sleeping with men and not knowing anything about them? Many women have lowered their standards just to have a man. Next, you have the women that only date; men with money. But what they don't know is, if you give your body away to quick. May I be candid concerning this matter? He's not going to give you anything except a wet behind; men like this usually come with the baggage of other women. It is becoming more and more apparent that women allow men to talk and treat them abusive. Their reasoning is they allow it so; they don't have to be alone. My God we have to do better! Here is another issue, stop sabotaging your life. If you have a man and you want to hold on to him. Please do not get pregnant STOP. This never works it will only push him away. However, he might take care of his baby if he is a quote on quote, stand up guy. Now if he is the type to say the child is not his, and try to insinuate you sleep around buckle up you're headed down a long bumpy road.

You will learn quickly with whom you're dealing with men usually say things like this to avoid taking responsibility. Scenarios, like this usually end up leading to resentment and issues for both parties. Due to pregnancy, our bodies change tremendously men who are genuinely head over hills in love even have a hard time adjusting to the change. I have heard men say they thought their wives were beautiful. However, they could not wait for their wives bodies to return back to normal. Here is another observation. Many women think by having sex that they are going to land their man's heart. In some cases, this could be a fact. But there is so much more to the story. Men want women with directions, substance and values that care about their reputations!

Men love sex and adventure but they want women who are loyal. I'm talking about real men now. They want women who have goals set. They love women who are determined who possess a true love for God. Why, because they know if you are a good girl they can trust you. They want a woman that's great. There is a lot to being a great woman take time to look inside your inner self. Women we have so much to offer if you do not agree. Then take action to make these statements line up! Step your game up! Take accountability for not being where you need to be in life and take steps to fix it. You must make sure you have a solid relationship with God; get in school exercise and keep your mind elevated. Read everything that you think will take you to the next level. In essence just be willing to achieve all you can. This is a classic example of what I was just expounding on in this next story.

One night I overheard some men speaking about how females, do not respect themselves. They said, "Females now days are easy when they call females the first thing they ask is where is the smoke or drink." One male ask the question, "Are females that stupid? He said, "Women can't come up with a better conversation?" Later ending with the response **what a turn off!** However, they did say they would go and smoke because they knew after wards it would be a definite go on sex. Now it seems they have branded most women as an easy lay with no direction. I do not think most men value nor respect women anymore. Well, the devil is a liar!!!! Ladies we have to do better listen years ago if a woman gave it up to easy she would be branded as community property. It has been my motto that before a man can make love to my body not only does he have to captivate me; he has to also make love to my mind.

One afternoon we were in exercise class a young lady said, "If I dresses conservative, I'm looking forward to a nice evening I'm not looking for anything risqué. However, if I put on a short skirt there usually is no application of panties." She went on to say this would be considered as her easy access night. **"Everything goes."** "HOUSTON, WE HAVE A PROBLEM!" "Noooo!" This is all wrong stop showing them everything; cover up and allow them to use their imagination. Listen there will be an appointed time to show him everything. One day I happened to be present while some men were having a conversation. One said, "I would rather be alone." I said, "That is not true." Another male spoke up and said, "Yes men say this deep but down in our hearts no man wants to be alone women are just easy and silly we get tired of dealing with, the same old nonsense women say they want to be respected but they don't give us anything to respect." Question did you know men felt this way? If not I'm so glad we covered it. Let's get back to Karen...

Chapter 7

Playboys and Players

Tim expects Karen to trust him Karen thinks "Is what I say, not important how come he acts as if he cannot hear me? If you're asking why, here is the answer if Tim listens to her he has to feel Karen and at this point, he clearly does not want to feel anything. He needs to remain numb if he opens up he may begin to catch feelings. This will cause him to start caring how things are going to make her feel. To Tim this is a no-no. This would make it difficult to play the field. Why is it in a relationship we don't want to see things that let us know the relationship is not good for us we just want to see the good. Answer: We have hope and want to believe facing the truth can hurt!

***

He can continue to make her think that she is nitpicky and crazy. Tim's now saying, "Karen is far from understanding. This is just what he wants her to think. **Karen is docile you would think she would be looked upon as Tim's dream. (Docile: means, eager to learn, teachable and submissive.) Instead Tim confused it with being, gullible, and stupid.** I have realized you should only be docile; for your husband. There are common sense rules for the dating scene. You need to be able to be in control of yourself. Always try to appear busy about business. Don't worry yourself or him, to death, calling him every five minutes and chasing him, **find you** something to do. Never allow him to make you feel like you need to be up under him all the time, because you don't! Not in that sense any way. What you do need is God, Air, Food, Water, Shelter, and Money.

Don't let him know! (Ladies you need your husband's okay). Always keep yourself appearing as if, you have it all under control. Because if you do not! He will use signs of weakness against you.

Ladies we should draw our strength from the word of God. "What the enemy meant for evil God will turn it for your good."

Genesis 50; 20 But as for you, ye thought evil against me, but God meant it unto good.

Women we have so much power! James Brown said some words. That were very strong he said "This Is a man's world!" By the second time he repeated these words I'm sure every man said. "Yes! This is a man's world! However, you cannot just stop listening there. Because then he said the most **POWERFUL** part, "That it would not be nothing; without a woman or a girl." Why, women bring forth the reproduction of mankind. We are the sweet fragrance of our men, and the relationships. You see men love to see the sway of a woman hips and the shine on her lips.

***

Lyrics taken from James Brown Album released in 1966

Never let him see you sweat learn this sentence "What a small thing like that never bothered me." Once while out to dinner. A guy I was dating began to speak about a young lady he had met he said she was pretty with an out cold figure. He mentioned all his friends wanted to sleep with her and pay him. I said, "Well is she any good?" Here is the deal it didn't matter whether he answered yes or no.

We would have had a problem he replied, "He didn't know and paused." I said, "Oh are you waiting on my response." he said, "Yes" I said, "Oh the small things never bother me and ordered desert." These words can be very effective when applied in the right sequence. You better believe things changed in our relationship. Every man desires companionship with someone who is compatible. They want a woman that when she walks in the room. Their hearts go pitter-patter and nearly stop. If he just considers you something to do. He will take you for granted. If he thinks for one minute that you are a push over that is exactly what he will do he will not only push you over he will walk all over you. The average woman desires to be in love. However, the idea of being in love is close enough for some. Once we fall for them, we tend to lose our identity in them with the thought I can change him by cooking for him sexing him etc.

FYI; **you can't change a man**. Some women's initial thoughts are if I pray God will change him and God can. But is it God's will? Everything lawful is not expedient. Stop telling yourself, "If I can make him happy we will be ok." No! Love yourself first and make you happy. It's called self preservation! Listen we have to stop giving ourselves to, someone who in return gives nothing. We have to start putting ourselves first (not over God) asking God to rebuild and restore everything. If a man or a woman is broken they can't effectively **give** love for real, we have to be made whole before we can truly love, someone else. If a man is broken and he still in love with someone else no matter how much you love him you have to realize if he doesn't love you, may need to put your big girl panties on and face it.

Hey he may not be the one! You need to know, if you choose to stay you will just end up dealing with lies, mind games, and heartbreak, that otherwise could have been avoided. It has come to my attention that if a man has done something wrong but he is not ready to accept responsibility. He will take the whole situation and before you know it he will turn it around and make you feel like you are the one at fault.

***Shay and Ken had been dating for some months. It was Ken's birthday so he said; "He wanted a special birthday Surprise." Shay responded, "Surprise like what?" He said, "It doesn't require any clothes." Shay said, "It's your birthday and I plan on rocking your world. She responded, "I going to give you every part of me tonight." She said, "She did and it was explosive. She said, "I did things that night I have never done." Shay said, "When they were done." He said, "That was **GREAT,** girl you wore me out." She said, "Girl I was all smiles like YES! I did that!" Then out of the blue he said "Babe I have to get early for work can you lock the door behind you? I'll call you later." Shay said, "It was about 5:30 in the morning. She said immediately, I went into shock after, I came out; I said "Ken I am your woman, how can you put me out, this time of morning?" Ken replied, "I didn't agree to that, we are just friends!" Shay said, "I quietly gathered my things and went home." She said, "I felt so stupid." Now let me explain what happened, Shay allowed herself to dream with Ken and believe his words. I want to spend the rest of my life with you, I want you to have my baby, I want to travel the world with you, I want the world to see us together."

The dreams he was selling were **pipe dreams**. You see he only shared his dreams with Shay only while they were having sex! Shay said "The next time we got together I let him know that I needed more." His reply was, "I am a single man and I am not ready for commitment." Shay let him know! "I am not something to do or something to screw!" Shay said, "I accepted the fact that he did not want to commit to me so, why couldn't Ken understand or, respect my point of view?" How is it he felt that Shay should not think enough of herself and not to want, to continue to sleep with him without, a commitment? Get this, not only did he want to have sex but, he wanted to have unprotected sex. Shay knew as a result from his actions that if she cut their sexual sessions off, he would leave her. Question she is a beautiful woman very intelligent that keeps herself together why couldn't he commit?

This could mean a relationship or marriage. Answer; because he did not want a decent woman. He wanted a party girl someone to get high with and drink alcohol. He needed someone loose that would not hold him to any kind of accountability. It was then that Shay decided that if Ken could not acknowledge her, she was not going to sleep with him. When Ken realized Shay was serious he got angry and said "I'm tired of you rejecting me and repeating yourself" You see she kept demanding commitment and holding back the sex. He said, "I heard you the last time." Anyhow, Shay would not sleep with him. She realized he was playing mind games. He let her know exactly where she stood. She had no grounds with him. Shay said, "I left his home around one AM, it took him until the next night to check, if I made it home." I believe this time she heard him! Shay got the point.

***Back in the day males were considered Playboys and Players. According to how many women they had sexual intercourse with. Let us examine the word playboy It is simple, he is still a boy and **He wants to play**.

1 Corinthians 13:11 says, [11]When I was a child, I spake as a child, I understood as a child, I thought as a child: but when I became a man, I put away childish things.

So, what are they pretend boys who grew into pretend men who thrives on being, make believe men? Their goal is to make you believe; everything they say. Have you ever heard a male say I am the man and according to the way he thinks; this is his truth. He is stuck he never grew up. Here is the deal he hasn't reached maturity. Therefore he is still operating out of foolishness. Ladies we do not need the brother that thinks they are the man.

We need that brother that is a Man.

But let me say this there is a difference in a man and a male. A man will sit his girlfriend down and let her know things aren't working out; he will suggest they take time apart. He will set aside just enough time for them to get their heads together. A man will know that bringing someone else in will only complicate things. A male/ boy would have to secure a new relationship. Why, because he doesn't know how to stand on his own.

A Man will tell you the truth; a boy will lie.

Being a man is not predicated on how long he can go in bed or how many ladies he can conquer. Nor can it be based on how bad he can beat you down.

Neither, can we equate it to the size of the muscle that resides in his pants. You must earn the right to be a man. Oh yes there is a process men have to take responsibility and be willing to make honest, quality, decisions. We as a people need to learn how to keep it real, and stand up when we have made bad decisions. However, not only do we need to stand up but we should be ready to take accountability. You see a fool will tell you he knows all. But be advised a Wiseman will listen, not being wise in his own eyes. The example of being wise is not the brother that feels he has the gift of knowing everything. A man should be prepared to humble himself and realize that what he knows is not all to be learned. He should be willing to take on a new mindset and become opened minded. Then it is quite possible that he could gain more knowledge and not just live life being a know it all!

Proverbs 1:5: A wise man will hear, and will increase learning; and a man of understanding shall attain unto wise counsels.

Chapter 8

Remain a Challenge

Because Tim works he tells Karen he cannot really afford the time to see her. Because he is too tired! Could it possibly be because she has given up everything (sexually)? It's safe to say this is no longer a challenge. Ladies make these men wait and work for everything. This is how you become a challenge. Trust me if his intentions are good he will appreciate you. We must always remember to remain a challenge until we figure out what his motives are. Let us review; He now has landed her heart. He has her undivided attention and her mind. What's left for him to conquer? **Nothing!** When it's all said and done. That's exactly what she will get **NOTHING!** You don't have to beg a man to spend time. People make time for the things they want. He will want to occupy your time. He won't allow you to miss him. Why because before you can he has already missed YOU. A **man** will do everything to maintain and keep his relationship.

If a relationship is not what he has in mind? You will just get excuses I am busy, let's take this slow. Keep in mind; he still wants to do everything that is done in a committed relationship just without the commitment. Here is the other side most women are serious about commitment. We will put our life on hold while most men aren't thinking about commitment; they are busy playing the field. Here is an old saying that most of our mothers used, be **a fool if you want to!** Most men have been labeled ignorant because most men know better but they don't do better. Now if a man does not knows better, than he would be considered immature and unlearned. Let's take a look at this situation it's simple he wants his cake and eat it too.

He is thinking I can get all the pleasures I want from her and when he craves for someone else. He can have you too. This is the deal women. You catch him hugged up with another woman. You can't say anything, because he will say, "Were just dating," **Sound wise? No!** We have been setting ourselves up for failure; for too long. Today is the day you learn. Question, what's your greatest investment? That's right you guessed it YOU. How can you expect someone else to invest in you, when you don't take pride in your own life? We have to learn how to empower ourselves. We must Change our thinking and find material and seminars that will stimulate our minds. We have to set goals for the future as a step to development our confidence. **Yes we have to develop our confidence**. We have to build our conversation skills and take time to discover our God given talents. You need to zero in on the things that make you feel that you're not worthy.

This will create away to not only figure things out, but it will help you to deal with the things that hinder you. You should wake up every morning and look in the mirror smile and say something kind to yourself. That's right! Learn to love yourself here are a few ways to take action. Remove yourself from around negative people. Next, the way you dress should scream success. When engaging in conversations with others always remain graceful. People tend to deal with you according to your appearance. Let's just say you are out and your hair is not done you have on a t-shirt and a pair of jeans. You are out and you are trying to sell something people will tend to over look you. Now, if you have on a nice pant suit or dress. People will be more prone to patronize you. But here is something to remember your appearance can make the difference between you becoming a success or becoming a failure.

You may not believe this but money attracts money so always dress the part and be willing to help others. Last but not least. You have to embody the fact that you are your, most **valuable** asset. You should set your market price above average. Here is how you raise your value take time and explore your options, for the best training available to help you pursue your accomplishment. After you complete the training and get the concept of your skill, keep working on it to make your skills better. If at first, it seems like you're not perfecting your skill don't quit remain consistent. Start believing in yourself and become your BIGGEST and best investor (Invest in yourself). Create different vehicles to reach all your financial goals.

Vehicles are the things that drive you to your financial goals. Exp: Your books, your new business etc. Always remain positive while on your journey; if you make a mistake remember everyone makes mistakes learn the lesson and move on. We have to learn what makes us feel good, and cause us to grow, then take a moment and figure out what our passions are and pursue them; while fulfilling our purpose. Remember there's nothing you can't achieve. Don't be afraid take a leap to acquire a CEO mentality. In doing so, we need to take the time and do research on any and everything that would put us in position to become our own boss. Always be willing to learn more spiritually and naturally pray the will of God over your life and set your life up, so you too can live your dream.

2 Timothy 2:15
Study to shew thyself approved unto God, a workman that needeth not to be ashamed, rightly dividing the word of truth.

We really have to know our worth and who we are. We need to learn how to set standards for what we will and will not except. Listen stop settling if it is not what you want. You do not have to accept it. However, in the process always remember to be realistic. You have to recognize the things that entail who you are, while you're working towards finding a healthy balance. I also need you to reflect, on things to help identify who you are and what it is you want. I need you to take a minute get a pen and paper and answer these questions. Who are you? What makes you happy? Do you really know what you will and will not accept? What makes you different? What do you need? What do you want? Do you know the difference? What do you do dream about? What's on the inside of you that you think about doing all the time? What are you passionate about? Now, here is some question how to gauge things and help you figure out the things you should not accept.

You first need to figure out what are things that make you uncomfortable as well as what angers or irritates you? You know that thing you promised yourself you would never take off anybody. Well those are the things that you should NOT accept in your life. Our dad should be the first male that sets the standards in our life. Yes, your first teacher should be your dad. Your dad should be the male from the start that teaches you the difference between a man and a boy? He should also teach how a man will be responsible and boy will want to play. They should instill in us that we are to be loved and adored. Our fathers should illustrate how men are purposed to be our protector. A father should be compelled to teach his daughter about respect, and as a result of serious conditioning, by no means will we accept any disrespect. Your dad should educate you, why you should respect yourself, and our moms should instill in us how to respect ourselves.

My Grandson was whining one night, this was some years ago. One of my many children (Wait let me explain this) for the record. I have many heartfelt extended children. However, I have three that I actually birthed, and a boat load of heart children. Well one of my extended sons told my Grandson. He said, "I told you about all that crying, I told you boys play, and Girls cry." Now women what do you think about that? Is this not what happens they play the field. We catch them cheating and they make us cry. Do you see how you can instill, something so subtly but so easily? At this time he was two years old being taught how the world says women or girls should be treated with disrespect. This is why it is important for fathers, brothers, and uncles to step in if the father is absent. We have to be taught to carry ourselves with respect.

They should share how men look at women, who do degrading things. They should also point out how men laugh at women; for degrading themselves. A lot of young women seek the love and attention from different men. As a result they hop from bed to bed as a replacement for the love they so desperately desired but, didn't receive from their fathers; due to imprisonment, death, or a lack of maturity. Early on I spoke about live wires here is another great illustration. The bible clearly teaches us that the man, he has purposed for, us will find us. Okay now I need you to be in position to be found and receive him. When the time arrives I need you to check for a few things like is their chemistry? How does he react when you make him angry? How does he respond when he is in pain, is he mean or does he act calm? If you guys are on bad terms will he talk through it or shut down? If tragedy strikes in your life or his life how does he respond? Is he supportive? Now this is just not about him, you have to ask yourself these same questions.

Because you have to be a part of the relationship he can't have his stuff all together, and you're a mess. Listen no one is perfect but you should be at the top of your perfection.

Proverbs 18:22 Whoso **findeth a wife findeth** a good thing, and obtaineth favour of the LORD.

At the tender age of six my dad was shot and killed. Needless to say for a six year old this turned out to have a heavy impact. I was the true definition of a daddy's girl. I just couldn't understand how something like this could happen. Shortly after this my life took a tragic turn. My mom married an abusive alcoholic who played a part in raising me. He would drink then when night would hit, he would creep in my bedroom. Let's just say he would try to do things a father should never do. This was my beginning of not trusting men. He was breaking my mom's trust while; tampering with mine. It was so confusing this man was saying he was my new dad **but my dad never crept in my room**. I was so disturbed it felt as though my father had abandoned me.

Something like this could ultimately release a spirit of rejection: in a young girl causing a yearning to be loved by a man! Any man! A situation like this can cause you to repeat the same situations over and over. While growing up I learned that the lessons that are not learned have to be repeated. I was never promiscuous but when I did connect with a man on a sexual level. It would be the equivalent of feeling loved. Why, because when you have sex, your body becomes one. If a person is gentle with you while having sex it could be looked upon as comforting. However, time and experience will teach you the difference between making love and just having sex. This is also the part when you learn men are conquers.

Listen up! Nine times out of ten a male will tell you, everything you want to hear during sex. "Oh, I love you this is mine! I'm not going anywhere." During this process we are thinking, "No this is my body!" By the time he is finished sad to say most women are saying, "Yes, I belong to you." Chances are once he gets up the whole conversation will change. What we need to understand is that they are telling us lies while being intimate. During sexual intercourse men tap into our emotions. By the time we get up were ready for **whatever**. Mean while we want to believe and do the things, he was saying, we were going to do during sex. The harsh reality is, when he gets up. (Literally) He will be telling you "WHAT EVER!" As a consequence, it will leave us **feeling**. Example (Women) Oh I was really feeling him.

Why did he act like that? On the flip side they will be **reacting** (Male). They'll be putting their shoes on grabbing their hats. Why, because the way most females dress cause men to lose their focus on their main objective. A Females dress/wardrobe can cause men to forget the true purpose of why God intended us to date. But check this out! A man will focus on you just to get you in bed. But here is the deal what a man truly wants to know is; is she worth holding on to once she gets out of bed? Are we compatible? Will she keep a clean house? Can she cook? This only applies if he looks at her like girlfriend material. But let's take a look at something a little different being equally yoked is the key to a strong; solid, lasting relationship. Unequally yoked, means you are connected with someone that has a different belief that's not on the same path. Here is the reason why being equally yoked; is important. It is already easy for the enemy to get into your relationship if you don't have it covered.

However, being a believer and dating a non believer opens the gate way, for the enemy to enter and reap havoc. I believe it's truly harder for those who dedicate their lives to prayer and fasting. The enemy's job is to sabotage the man why because the man is the head. The head controls the body, meaning he can destroy the whole house. A man not lined up in the will of God is open to attack whether it is lust for money, women, alcohol or drugs. The devil will bombard him with temptations. This is why he cannot just pick any woman; he has to have a praying wife that is in tune with God, equipped with prayer that will not have a problem, fighting in the spirit and covering him daily. Now, if you are a woman and you are in church and you marry a man who is not in church. If church is not his interest trust me you are going to have a much harder time. Why, because light and darkness have no fellowship. Leaving him prey for the devil. Therefore, the man will not be receptive; to the Holy Spirit or to God's word. Your mate may say I want to celebrate let's go to the night club and have a drink. You may be thinking its Friday night service at the church we should go there. It is going to be hard to reach a happy medium.

Proverbs 1:7

The fear of the LORD is the beginning of **knowledge**: but fools despise wisdom and instruction.

2 Corinthians 6:14

Be ye not unequally **yoked** together with unbelievers: for what fellowship hath righteousness with unrighteousness and what communion hath light with darkness?

Chapter 9

I Mastered the Art

I mastered the art of how to be a man pleaser. In life we base our life situations on being pleasing to people. If it's one thing I knew that, I was good at it was how to please a man. One day I began to think the way I go out my way to please man. I thought if I just applied my skills to please God, how much better my life would be. We have to possess a healthy relationship with ourselves (love ourselves). Before were able to build a well rounded relationship. We must be able to build ourselves up, so that no matter what we can go out in the world possessing knowledge and still function. How many times, have we found ourselves in situations where we say I'm not happy? How many times have you found yourself holding on to something that wasn't there?

Yet, we stay knowing the person is not healthy for us. Questioning ourselves "Is he ever going to, change." Hoping for the best but expecting the worst. Have you ever noticed that when he is wrong. He is quick to tell you he's sorry? But his actions remain the same. Take a stand! This is the part where you say I love you but **I love me more**. Take one minute and assess your relationship. Remember what we speak is what we create. Think about what you have been speaking concerning your life. Have you been saying, "I'll never find someone to love me? I feel I'm not good enough or are you saying Lord, I am waiting on my Boaz" Which is something you shouldn't be speaking. Because he belonged to Ruth! "You see we have to learn. To speak what we want into existence. Then begin to Thank God! Here is what you should be speaking.

I thank you for the man that you tailor made just for me. Just like when you created Boaz with Ruth in mind. Thank you lord for my husband who loves me like Christ loved the church.

Death and life are in the power of the tongue. Proverbs 18:21 **Death** and **life** are in the power of the tongue: and they that love it shall eat the fruit thereof.

So, we have to speak it and Thank God! Be patient wait on God and watch it manifest. Well, you might be wondering how do you apply these skills? It's easy by spending time with God and communing with him. We have to learn to discipline ourselves. Read and study the word in order to be pleasing to God! Just as we have learned how to please our men. We have to become intimate with God. We must Serenade God with love songs not ever nagging, nor complaining giving him all we have to offer. You should be mindful of God even in your day to day conversation. Always remaining available open and honest to God.

Knowing that God would never take you for granted. It's an amazing feeling knowing you are in good standings with God. You can bear all before God not worrying about what he is expecting from you, not having to wonder do I meet his approval. *(like you do with man).* I mean who has the time for emotional roller coasters. Today he wants to be with you. Tomorrow he says I need time to get myself together. He is being indecisive. Choose God! He will be everything you need him to be. Don't you dare let anyone tell you anything different? Being connected to God is a Blessing! You can not only count on God but you can depend on him. Whenever you call (pray) he's going to answer the love he holds for you us unconditional.

Hebrews13:8
Jesus Christ the same **yesterday**, and today, and forever.
Hosea 4:6
My people are destroyed for lack of knowledge: because thou hast rejected knowledge.

This story happened a while ago my friend said he wanted to introduce me to his mom. I was like cool! Now I'm in a position to see what's on the inside of him? Yes I get to see what kind of man I am dealing with. Watch how a man treats his mother; it is a sure indication of how you can expect to be treated. Do not take my word follow him home. Also how his family and friends treat you are predicated on how he treats you get this, if he treasures you, no one will get out of line with you not without a fight. So, back to meeting his mom, we get to her house at first, he treated her nice then I overheard him using profanity directed at her so, I asked, "Why do you disrespect your mom?" He said, "Because she does dumb things." I cut my losses quick because, I knew it wouldn't be long before he would be disrespecting me.

*** This young lady named Mary was married to Edgar. His family was always disrespectful. One day at a family function one of Edgar's family members tried to fight her she said she could hear them saying, "Why she always hanging around we don't like her! His girl looks way better than she does." His wife became furious and said,

"Enough is enough" I don't like you either! In the heat of the moment his cousin threw a bottle and hit her. That's when Edgar stepped in, and he and his cousin began to fight which led to a major divide in the family. Now if he had given her the proper respect that was due. None of this would have taken place. **Now back to Karen**....

Chapter 10

Don't You Dare Settle

Karen spends time with Tim never does she complain about how they do not go to the park anymore or why don't they go to restaurants anymore. Instead she always lets Tim know whatever you want to do is fine as long as were together. Karen could adjust. How could Tim have not seen this? Karen is settling!

I can recall being in a store contemplating which juice I should get the selection was very limited. It was hot and I was thirsty my thoughts were to just grab anything. The person I was with said, "Don't get that you can clearly see that is not what you want why you are settling?" Question, how many times have we found ourselves asking? How did I find myself here? Sound familiar? Reason! Because the conditions of our lives today are based upon the decision we made yesterday.

In addition the decision we made yesterday always constitutes how our relationships are structured. The problem is, if we keep making yesterday decisions today, then our tomorrow will keep looking like yesterdays. If you ask the average female what they desire. The desire in their heart is often not reflected in whom they are dating or attracted to. Why, because of the flesh it will trick us into settling. Paul said, "Only through the Holy Spirit can we get free from the bondage of our flesh. New mindsets will renew us; our old mindset enslaves us. Making us become captive to our old selves. Have you ever wondered why, every relationship you were in the men treated you the same?

That's because they were the same men; just in different bodies. My ex would always tell me that lipstick/ lip-gloss made me look ugly. Every time I would doll up, he would frown up. Later he told me that, when I dressed up I would look good to him instead of saying you look amazing he chose to frown.

*** One evening Candy came over so my daughter could do her hair. Her ex called and said, "What are you doing?" Candy replied, "Just finishing up getting my hair styled." You could tell Candy was happy he had called. Candy could not wait to get to him so, he could see her. So, when she got home. He was outside waiting for her, this was his response, he asked, "Why did you put that bull crap in your hair?" Now you look just like your mom. He said this to tear Candy down. After hearing this, Candy called me very upset and told me what he said. I said, "Let me speak to him:" I asked "What exactly does that mean? He kind of snickered and replied "What that she looks like her mom?"

So my reply was, "Did you mean like an old woman or like an Indian." He started laughing and said "No, she looks pretty like an Indian; I just was not expecting her to look like that!" Yeah right! So, what was he expecting? Sometimes, it is not what you say it is how you say it. This is a true example of how the enemy deceives men into tearing women down. This is why you have to be confident in whom you are, don't continue to allow people to make you; feel like your less than. You have to know that you are somebody. Ladies you don't need anyone to make you happy. Happiness comes from within; this is why I keep reiterating about you loving you. Listen you should get your life so together that if someone attempts to enter into your life.

It becomes exciting after it hits you that the only thing they can do, is add to your life. I've learned through many experiences that no matter what type of relationship it is. You have to be careful with whom you allow in your life. Even in relationships with friends, we can find ourselves settling. Now if I had not questioned him Candy would have immediately went home and taken her hair down. Something so traumatic should challenge us, never to allow anything make you doubt yourself clearly this is not what happens. We have to learn to trust God for our mate but we don't, somehow we end up reaching right down and grab the brothers, that are all tore up; to clean him up and mend his wounds. You would think that would be the end of it but, no you then have to wait on him, to figure out what it is that he wants to do. He needs to figure out whether he is ready to serve God or not, this process can be overwhelming.

Please if you can't wait on God to send him then you need to allow God the time to clean him up. Here is a word to the wise. You cannot change a man but what you can do is, work on yourself and remain focused; keeping your options open. Because the one you're waiting on has free will and **may not be willing to change**. Here is an eye opener to help you avoid unnecessary grief. God loves us and he wants the best for us. God indeed is a teacher. he wants us all to depend on him. I can remember going through a rough spot after a break up. The people I leaned on for support, that I prayed with disappeared. My state of mind became very weary. Here is a **Key**; at this point this is where you should pay attention. Sometimes God will isolate you so he can have your undivided attention. Here is where God puts you in a position to be conditioned to hear his voice. He will begin, to remind you of the things he was showing you. While letting you know, that if you had of paid attention you wouldn't be in your predicament.

Through this process he will begin to teach you. It's up to you to get the lesson. **ATTENTION** after every course there will be a test. If you didn't pay attention to the teacher (**God**) and you don't pass the test. Whatever you went through will be repeated. Here is another life lesson. I had to learn to surround myself with people who have like minded dreams and visions. There were people who I was with day-to-day. Whom I shared my dreams and visions; bad decision let me tell you why. My visions cause them to evaluate their life and face their inadequacies. They told me I couldn't be great. They said, "We don't know why you won't go get a real job." You are wasting time sitting on that computer." They started finding all sorts of reasons to criticize. It was not until, God revealed to me stop sharing my vision.

This is when I realized I could be great but, I had to shut my mouth. But the sad part is I only revealed my vision to people that I was close to, that I felt would support it. The hard reality was my vision was so, great that some couldn't handle it. Be mindful of who share your dreams with one more thing, if it takes too long for your dream to materialize; prepare for a lot of people to leave you. Listen and that's okay because God will replace every last one of them that left. Remember Joseph made the mistake of sharing his dream and I'm sure he never thought it would cost him everything for that season.

Genesis 37: 5And Joseph dreamed a dream, and he told it his brethren: and they hated him yet the more.

Relationships can be hurtful! I'm talking about relationships whether they are friendships or intimate. Sometimes we believe people are our friends and we become too comfortable, not being mindful.

However, everyone around you is not out to get you sometimes, God has to move you away from people so he can birth the vision he has placed in you. I get questioned a lot as to why guys treat their girlfriends so cruel. Well, here is one reason people will criticize and tear you down, to make them feel better another would be it's a learned behavior or he watched his father treat his mother that way. The most common reason usually is you could be the side chic.

I try to be very discerning and trust me I do not let everyone in my circle. Sometimes it is hard to spot those that don't belong in your life. Always be mindful; with whom you share your life. Stay positive, alert and, operate in discernment there are a lot of negative people who don't want to see you succeed. Yes, this is why you have to keep your landscape of life maintained, meaning you have to keep beautifying and cut the grass; or you will never see the negative people. This is why we have to be THANKFUL when God closes Doors for us. Think about it most times we don't know how to close them. Whether it is relationships, jobs, opportunity or ventures that you thought were good for you. Remember, God knows best you might not understand it. Hey it might even hurt. **Trust and Thank God.**

Matthew 7:6 Don't cast your pearls before swine. Give not that which is holy unto the dogs, neither cast ye your pearls before swine, lest they trample them under their feet, and turn again and rend you.

****

I encountered a young woman named Mary that met a guy. When she met him he had two pairs of underwear a couple pairs of jeans his trade was a street mechanic.

Mary took interest in him and started buying him clothes. She began to refer customers that needed their cars serviced. Mary then went a step further and did the number one no- no she gave birth to his child in hopes to keep him. You couldn't have told her, she didn't have the key to his heart. Mary sent him to school and paid his full tuition. I promise you! It wasn't long, before he started acting out of character. He started being verbally abusive and staying out all night. Right after graduation he moved out and married another woman. She was Angry and that wasn't the worst part she suffered a nervous breakdown. We need to learn to become; angry at the source. We have to become angry at the enemy for the way he sends his little assignments to treat us. Sometimes men and women are sent by the enemy with a **soul** purpose to destroy lives. Have you ever thought? "Where did he come from?" Then realized he had to be a distraction; sent on assignment. Well nine times out of ten they usually are.

John 10:10 The thief cometh not, but for to **steal**, and to **kill**, and to **destroy**: I am come that they might have life, and that they might have it more abundantly.

The bible speaks about the rich man, beggar man and the dog. So, when a man would approach me regarding sex. I would get offended and angry my thoughts were all men are dog's especially when I discerned their agenda was sex. Today, I have a better understanding of men's nature and how they operate. Study and interaction taught me how to effectively deal with men on a day to day basis. All though life challenges, caused me to lose my way, just as the prodigal son left home. I too moved out of my purpose. You see his father was rich and adored him; much like my father in heaven is rich and adores me. Although he did not adore my foolishness!

The prodigal son wanted a different experience. In the long run he took life for granted. He wanted to go out an experience life. He was out there exploring life and used; all his inheritance. Leaving him to eat and live with the pigs. This is so crazy! I found myself in the exact same situation. Oh but one day he came to his self, and so did I we both said, "I know who my father is and we changed our situation." You see he didn't have to live like that and nor did I. He said, "I'm going home and so did I."

Luke 15 [17]And when he came to himself, he said, How many hired servants of my father's have bread enough and to spare, and I perish with hunger! You see we as women need to come to ourselves. I too found myself in ungodly situations. This is why we should become offended by, the things some men are trying to offer. We do not have to sit under the table and beg like a beggar man for the crumbs.

Luke 16 [20]And there was a certain beggar named Lazarus, which was laid at his gate, full of sores, [21]And desiring to be fed with the crumbs, which fell from the rich man's table: moreover, the dogs came and licked his sores.

What are the crumbs? Accepting men that treat you like the only thing you're good for is sex. Keep in mind this only happens (sex). When he decides to makes time for you. It has to be a rude awakening to suddenly realize you are dealing with a mate who does not appreciate you, nor respect you. If you need proof watch how he treats the things; that are important to you? Example: If you have a car he will use it but he won't do any maintenance or keep it clean. That's a flag! You better believe he's not into you. The way you think he is.

You see you my friend you are their just for his use. Ladies we add great value, we are of a rare quality. We must realize our worth don't you know, we are very useful regarding life WE CAN PRODUCE LIFE! I am a woman of God with integrity! Ready for my feast the lord has prepared I want all the trimmings. I do not know about you but this sister wants it all. I don't just want a slice of bread I want the whole loaf. We should never have to convince a man what are worth is. I demand to be respected, adored, cherished, loved, and appreciated. I want the ring, marriage, and stability I want a relationship that consists of substance that's meaningful and solid. I want a man equipped with quality and consistency. Listen I need a mate that operates in these principles. **Seems like a lot right**? Well it's not you deserve much more.

1 Corinthians 11:8
For the man **is** not of the **woman**: but the **woman** of the man.

Women we should never lose our voice our opinion should always be viewed as important. First, thing you must remain consistent. In order for a change to be made it must be a mutual agreement. Longevity and precedence should be essential in one another's life. The both of you should always be willing to always explore love till the end of time. The bible declares that the man is the head (Husband). His job is to cover you meaning he should be responsible, equipped, and ready to take the lead. However with that being said, he should be the man that doesn't mind facing off with the enemy. A man endowed with a mindset to protect. He should be someone concerned about your mind, body, and soul a praying man that's steadfast and unmovable. A man so infused with power that if the devil dares to try and magnify his attack.

Your mate's prayers would apply pressure to the enemy, and block every assignment. He should be a true provider, with a back bone who is connected to you emotionally and has your back.

1 Corinthians 11:3
But I would have you know, that the **head** of every **man is** Christ; and the **head** of the woman **is** the **man**; and the **head** of Christ **is** God.

Jeremiah 17:9 The heart is **deceitful** above all things, and desperately **wicked**: who can know it?

 The heart wants what it wants as a result we tend to settle. This often causes us to make bad decisions. We must take control of our emotions or they will take control us and rule our situations. My mother once asked, "Could you not go across the alley and get a man." She furthered her conversation by saying, "Just because he is from your neighborhood and shows you attention does not mean he is the one she continued, "You should all ways keep yourself together you should frequent upscale events and venues. Venues that have laid back relaxing atmospheres. She also would say, "Hey you never know when or where you are going to meet your Mr. Right." I now understand what she meant. We have choices! Here is another observation people accept less, because they don't know there's more.

****One night we were sitting around; having girl talk. It was Toya, Kiki, and I. Toya began to tell her story about how she was dating a married man. She said, "He always invites me to his home to fulfill his sexual desires for pay." So Ki-Ki said, well where is his wife while all this is going on? Toya said, "On vacation at work etc.

He always makes me comfortable, and I always feel safe, you see he puts the alarm on to ensure our safety In case she comes home unexpected. Then we go to the **basement** and have sex." Toya, let us know that this was not personal but, this was business. So, Ki-Ki said "You mean you two have sex in that woman's home." Toya replied, "Yes girl I do not care." In response Ki-Ki, said, "Yeah but you should" Ki-Ki furthered her comments by saying, "Girl you should have told him I am about to give your wife something; you do not." Toya said, "And **WHAT** is that?" Ki-Ki replied, "RESPECT!"

****

A male was expounding on how he had multiple women. One was coming through the front door and another was going out the side door. He said if they would have caught him. He said, "It would have been a relief." He simply had too many women. His motto was women come a dime a dozen. As quick as one left another was coming. He said,
 "Women aren't hard to replace all I have to do is pull up in a nice car flex my jewelry and my money." So I sat there for a moment then I asked, "Why do you feel this way?" He responded, "Women are shallow, money hungry, easy, stupid, and needy." Ladies! LISTEN, because a man has jewelry, money, and a car doesn't mean you should sell yourself short. Don't allow them to make a spectacle of you. Here is the deal when it's all said and done it's his cars, and his money; not yours! Concentrate on you! Not on what a man has or what he has to offer. Our focus should be based around finding ways, to advance **our lives.** I can't express how important it is to love you.

Here are a few tips always keep yourself together. Treat yourself with dignity and respect and always carry yourself like a lady. Never loud and abrasive, always soft and settle. You should also find ways to communicate without using profanity and by all means please don't come out, with your hair all over your head not bathed. Seriously, how could a man take interest? Date with a purpose (Marriage). We need to bring back the principles of old fashion courting. Which consist of him asking you out on a date? Then he must give you a few days notice allotting you time to get everything together. Here are a few things we should incorporate back into our preparations, before the date take a long hot bubble bath. If your bottom half is heavy soak it and please don't neglect to use feminine hygiene products. If you are top heavy the same principles apply. Yes apply deodorant under your breast if you have experienced smelling musk in those areas. Take time with your hair and makeup, make sure your nails are neat and your feet are done.

 Pick out an outfit that flatters your shape but will still cause him to use his imagination. Set rules and guide lines tell them you only date men who still believe in chivalry? When he arrives to picks you up, he should come to the door with flowers in hand. Next, he should open your car door during the ride there should be a discussion before you arrive to your destination. It should be established **NO** cellar devices during dinner and ladies always remember the essentials courtesy, respect and honesty. There should never be a problem communicating. You should be able to have a stimulating conversation. However in today's society that's not happening, most females try to stimulate men sexually. They use diversion tactics in hopes to cover up the fact that they can't hold an intellectual conversation.

Enough is enough! Go back to school stop using your body as a tool. Also never assume anything regarding relationships. Ask questions where do I stand in your life? Are **we** committed to **one another**? I found out that people are sleeping together and sharing homes without any commitment. Come on ladies let's get it together! Then you have the female that lacks confidence. They can't figure out why men only come around and tell them what they want to hear; just to sex them. Listen you have to carry yourself, in such a way that men feel they need to be a part of your world.

Never carry yourself like what's wrong with me? Why can't I get a man? Men say this is a complete turn off. Respect is important, did you know people learn how to treat you by the way you treat yourself? Learn to treat yourself like you're a special occasion, therefore when people enter your life they will know to cheer and celebrate you. If you think about it everyone appreciates a special occasion... Remember to always carry yourself like you are worthy to be a man's wife. Always have an upbeat attitude never present yourself as a Debbie downer. Here is another key a smile is better than a frown. When you head out into the world ladies put your shades on apply that lip gloss hold your head up and smile. The world is yours...

Chapter 11

You Sure Know How to Pick Them

As I look back on almost everything my mom and I did were life lessons. I can remember as a little girl my mom would take me to the race track. Where she would bet on horses based on how they were bred or their color their name and track records. I can remember how excited she would become when she would win. We would watch the horses anxiously as the gate would open sometimes the horse would not even come out. Because the horse was, stagnate. Question, have you ever dealt with a man that did not want to move forward or change? Here is the equivalent there were horses that would come out full speed get half way there and turn around and go back. Some men will confess their love to you just to trick you into believing that you are the one.

The moment marriage and commitment are mentioned. They become gripped with fear. Then you have men that will stay in relationships that are not healthy. These men will tell their friends and family how unhappy they are in one breath and in the next breath, he will tell her he is ready for commitment. What's happening is they really don't want to come out of their comfort zone. A man will come out of a relationship thinking he's never going back but will return back. Why, because although the world is study evolving they don't want to conform to change. Sometimes the horses would come out and dance around because in their mind this is a game. To some guy's relationships are games they're not looking for a serious relationship. Some horses come out at a smooth even pace and flow to the finish line.

Yes, this horse is the equivalent of a man that would be marriage material. Now, there is a man that's in love and knows what he wants. We really need to analyze our relationships from the beginning. It appears to be safe to say, that some women are easy now days. The fear of being alone causes women to ignore red flags. Let's become accountable to one another and fix this. One day some friends and I were talking one asked? "What do you think the reason is why people wait so long to divorce?" She questioned, "What are they waiting on?" My response was, "Fear of change." There are times even though we are not happy we stay in relationships knowing we have the capability to change. However stepping out and acting on it is considered growth even though change can and will sometimes cause pain.

Sad to say but we have all been conditioned to look forward to negativity. However, you can't always look for the negatives in situations. If you do this it will open the door for fear to come in. Have you ever found yourself? Holding on to something that wasn't there? Questioning... What if he enters in to a new relationship and treats her right? These are things we deal with in break ups and would be regarded as growing pains. This is exactly how we find ourselves thinking we are comfortable in uncomfortable situations.

**** 2 Timothy 1:7 For God hath not given us the **spirit** of **fear** but of power, and of love, and of a sound mind. Life is change! We must learn to operate in the things of God appling them to our everyday lives. We must continue to eat the word of God just as we eat natural food. We should eat so much of the word that we get so fat that the devil; cannot move us.

****2 Corinthians 5:17 Therefore if any man be in Christ he is a new creature: **old things** are passed away; behold, all **things** have become new.

Chapter 12

Master Deceivers

Are we really living or just merely existing? Are you feeling like you are barely here without a purpose. When you should be living; fulfilling your destiny. We should never take one second of our life for granted. Every second that passes is **gone forever**. We as women should always. Operate with integrity and morals. Never thinking it' cool to operate with a lot of different men. We need to choose to have one man in the event, that if anything takes place such as a STD or a baby is conceived you're not found at fault. Cases such as this have been known to cause a collapse in the relationship. Ladies if your relationship isn't working. The best thing to do is not to play mind games or retaliate just let it go.

***

One of my extended sister's named Amy called she was so; excited she said, "I met a man and it's so refreshing we have been seeing each other for a while now and you know, I was wondering because he has remained a perfect gentleman. Not once has he made a sexual advance toward me." She went on to say, "We have spent the night together on a few occasions which made me question his authenticity." Yeah sad right! I know we have so many down low brothers. He told Amy, "He was only interested in going to dinner and going to the movies." His words were "I'm different!" He wanted to take it slow and show Amy what he really consisted of. If there is something you really want to know about someone if you listen to him or her long enough what they consist of will be revealed.

I said, "Sweetheart that is the overlay for the under play." I said, "What he is doing is setting his own stage. He is telling you, I am not interested in your body. I respect you too much." This was the drill ladies he was making love to her mind or, shall I say he was trying to screw with her mind! So the next move was supposed to be on Amy he expects her to say I know you respect me. Listen, we are both grown! You have proven yourself to me and to show you how much I appreciate you, I want to make love to you. I said, "Girl if it does not play out like this I truly want to know." We laughed and Amy said, "Ok." A few days later she called me saying, "Girl you were right he called me." This is how the conversation went he said, "When you get sexually frustrated what do you do?" Amy said, "Since I am not married I quote the scripture this too shall pass." Amy said so; she asked him, "When you get frustrated, what do you do?" He replied, "Well you know I have two hands."

He said, "You know I have been thinking since we have come to know one another we could just use one another." Amy asked, "What happen to your vow of Celibacy?" Remember earlier I spoke about men dropping the ball. Well ladies, here is another good example. He dropped the ball now Amy is making her exit while throwing up the **Deuces**. Who knows if he had just been honest they could have gone a lot further. Sometimes we as women are over qualified for relationships. I have always heard that women were always more mature than men. This doesn't mean you have to dummy yourself down as a woman. If he appears he doesn't want to get it right, just understand that particular man wasn't ready hang on in there he's coming. Your life should exude I may not be perfect, but I will be the best thing that ever happened to you.

Remember to always embrace the cycle of being a woman. Sometimes we have to USE our weakness as a plus embracing your limitations; for instance. I know I cannot go toe to toe with a man physically; but if we study them long enough. We can get with them mentally if you are a woman there is no sense of you trying to fight a man. Just use wisdom and your feminine whiles. However, you should be able to diffuse an argument and still get your point across. The key to this is always remaining a lady. This is something that's not easy if you're emotions are all over the place you still have to remain focused. Now this doesn't apply if you recognize you are dealing with a master deceiver. Why? A master deceiver wants to gain full control so he can falsely mislead and persuade you.

He will conquer every woman you know in your face; while pretending he loves you. He will convince you that there is no man that can hold a candle to him. He will assure you his love is pure while taking you for everything you have; his plight is to be a counterfeit contender, and a great pretender. **Great pretenders** are master deceivers. These men will walk out of your life and they will leave you for dead, to them I guess you are dead but know this God will resuscitate you! Contenders are people that are in competition that will do anything to deceiving you into believing they're the one, signs to watch out for is settle deceit. Their goal is to always be in a position to control you.

Example:

They will know you are coming but tell you when you're on your way to call. This is so they can have their timing down to a science. They then will call their other females to continue to make them feel like they are the one.

He will speak warm kind words that make you just melt. He will do things like when he has company. He will send her to the store just, to be able to call you and tell you. That he's tired and turning in early and he just needed to hear your voice. Meanwhile, if the other woman comes back too quickly if he thinks the woman on the phone can hear her when she comes in he will tell her, "I have family coming in I'll call you back when they leave." Another example would be a man will try to convince you, that you are the only one BUT, he needs you to understand that he is busy; this is because he needs to be able to check on all his females. He'll text you to make you feel secure and to learn your location while keeping up with what you are doing. Once he is with you, he will text them.

Think about it! I have heard men refer to this as checking their traps. You know what they say when the cats away the mouse will play. Once this kind of man gets hold to your heart; consider yourself trapped. But here is the thing. Sometimes, you have to allow them to believe you don't have a clue; to what's going on. Don't you know being a woman come with perks. We are gifted with women's intuition, prayer, power and discernment. These ingredients form a Powerful Dangerous Woman take the time to ask questions that you clearly know the answers to. However, when you ask questions it is imperative that you look them in their eyes; this should be done to see their expression. You should also learn their different expressions so; you will know whether they are being dishonest or sincere.

Chapter 13

Divide and Conquer

I was speaking with a gentleman he told me that most men have a main objective (divide and conquer). I found in so many cases men will try to lure you away from friends and family. They will create division between you and your family if you allow them, they will destroy every relationship you have. If its friendship he will say, "There is just something about her I just do not like. I have heard about her, you should not be keeping company with her. People are going to begin to label you too. You need to be a leader." They will say anything to cause separation.

If its family they'll say your mom or dad is trying to run your life or they are trying to keep you in a child like mentality. Your people just don't want you to grow up. If it works, it makes it a little bit easier for him to find your inconsistency and weakness. So he can take his time without interruptions and chip away at your self-esteem, until he breaks you, putting him in full control to run things. He also told me that men compliment women and according to how they receive their compliments. They can determine if she has L.S.E (Low Self-Esteem) men like this look for women that are vulnerable. They seek women that don't feel good about their selves or appear to be needy. Example: if he tells her that she is pretty and in reality, if she thinks she is just a little below average. If she replies,
  "Really" and smiles too much this is a clear indication that she has LSE.

This is where the process will begin; he will make her feel like she is the prettiest girl in the world. Once he is confident that she has bit the bait he will begin to degrade her and break her. Next, subject, be careful with men and their phones. I know that sex is purposed for marriage. I also know that everyone is not operating on biblical principles. Never, allow your partner to pick up their phone during intimacy. I don't care if he says your beauty captivates me or, he just wants to see your expressions. Never allow him to so call turn on the light. Take it from me you will be recorded. I don't care if he is a long time boyfriend or your fiancé. Never allow it! Don't let him convince you to take pictures of your body parts. I don't care how many times he tells you that he won't show anybody. Unless this is a Husband wife thing! **Even with that you have to be careful**. There have been numerous occasions women have trusted men and they have betrayed them. Here is something else females send nude pictures to their men, and they send them to their friends. I have been present and actually seen them show their sacred pictures to others.

***

One night this young woman sent naughty pictures to her boyfriend and he put them on a website because he found out that she dated one of his friends. He said he did it to teach her a lesson. Get this! She didn't know he even knew the other guy. It was no excuse for his behavior. She could have ended up in a very awkward situation. What if her mother and father lived out of town and end up with a forwarded email? Wouldn't that be awful!

***One evening

Rodney and Shawn were hanging out Rodney asked Shawn, to use his phone .While he was using his phone Rodney was going through it, he was looking at pictures of Shawn's girlfriend not only did he look at her pictures. He sent them to his phone. **Major violation** these pictures were for Shawn's eyes only when he finished he erased them out of Shawn's sent messages. Well Rodney's girl friend saw the pictures and flew off the handle.

She immediately began to call Shawn's girl friend a home wrecker she even tried to fight her, when everything calmed down and the truth was aired out imagine everyone's surprise when they found the real culprit. Beware not all smiling faces mean you well.

****Next story is about a sixteen year old that experienced life way too early that went by the name Puddin! Now this young girl was very beautiful she had an hourglass figure and a promising future. By the age of sixteen she became pregnant by a man who was twice her age. Now Puddin's mom was bedridden and as a result of this her mom could not keep a watchful eye on her. Puddin's dad had been brutally murdered. So, this made it easy access for the enemy to reap havoc. His name was Rueben! Reuben was at least fifteen years her senior. His age alone put him in a position to get a hold on her and cause major damage. Puddin never stood a chance. Rueben was thirty plus years old and a married man with children. She found out quick but not soon enough that he didn't mean her any good. In any event, by the time she realized. What she had gotten herself into, she had given birth to his child and pregnant again.

Now someone might say she should not have been messing with a married man. Puddin was sixteen fatherless with a mother that was bed ridden. This would be the best-case scenario for; Divide and Conquer. However, there are women who are far more mature and have gotten eaten alive. Let us take a look she is sixteen this man is telling her that he can be her protector and he can also provide for her (Much like a father figure Huh). In all reality, he was a wolf in sheep's clothing! In the course of their relationship Puddin met and start dating Tony a young handsome entrepreneur that showed he had good intention for pudding. One night while they were out on a date Tony said, "Over the course of time I have became very fond of you and I want to marry you. Will you marry me?" Puddin said "Yes" Now Puddin's mom was excited about this young man, she felt this would be her daughters escape. Prior to this she told Rueben to leave her daughter alone. He gave his word. That he would but he didn't. Puddin told Rueben what Tony said?

So Rueben replied "I'm coming to get you we need to talk." He came by and picked her up took her to the river Rueben said "b****!... If I can't have you nobody can." He pulled his pistol and blew her brains out. Then without any thought threw her in the river keep in mind her daughter, was six months old and Puddin was six weeks pregnant. He then went home and told his wife. "You do not have to worry about that... b**** any more. I killed her! Take my clothes to the alley, and **burn** them NOW! I'm going to take a bath." She replied, "Okay!" Then his wife called Puddin's mother and told her all that had happened. She then reported her husband to the police. Now, how can this be when this man is clearly married?

Some men feel once they have slept with a woman, it entitles him to have control and owner ship over her. Somehow, he believes that she in fact, is his property. What Rueben failed to realize is that he could never have a real relationship with his Child. In that instance Rueben destroyed lives the infant child will grow up and never know her mom. When the infant thinks of her father she will think of him as the man that took her mother's life. The wife has to deal with the fact that not only is her husband an Adulterer but he is a Murderer. His children by his wife will now grow up; without their dad. His unborn will never know life... Poor Puddin! Her life was much like her unborn she never had a chance. How dare Puddin think she can move on to have a better life.

Chapter 14

Now That's Presentation

Karen is now in a state of despair her emotions are all out of control. She realizes that all the things Tim is feeding her are not getting her full thus, she cries out to Tim. Karen tells him lately she has been feeling somewhat lonely Karen knew that communication was key, so she began to plan her method of how she would communicate with him. Keys* First you speak how you feel to your partner. I would like to clarify something if you are in an intense argument and you both are yelling. You may as well end your conversation; neither will hear nor see the others point of view resulting in someone saying, "I really didn't mean to say that I was angry, you know I didn't mean it!" Okay here is one of the most important factors, presentation is everything. Next, chose your choice of delivery and make sure your delivery is smooth.

So, that he will be able to digest it and then allow him time to process it. This will create the opportunity to present your case and receive his response so, that you both may be able to see the big picture. Here is an example when you fix your mates plate. You want the meal to look appealing so, you are going to make sure that the food is carefully arranged. So, if you have baked spaghetti with cheese you would sprinkle parsley flakes for, the visual effect and serve it hot. This is the presentation when he eats it. You will know if the food was good or not. He is either going to eat all of his food or mess over it. Either way it would be considered his response. Just food for thought! Not only do we need to be able to effectively communicate but we have to be able to think for ourselves.

***One night, some of my people were out at a party. Different guys kept rolling up in these new cars. The young girls were hopping in and out. Now, this is the deal the guys were driving stolen cars. Here is what happened! A young nice looking brother name Chad pulled up on a young woman named Trina she said; "He had a very nice car." I believe Trina said it was a challenger she stated he was very handsome, well groomed, well spoken, and nicely dressed. He asked her could he call her sometimes. Trina said "Yes" they exchanged numbers. They talked for hours on the phone; for about a month. He asked, "Trina can I take you out?" She said, "Yes" He took her to dinner. However, after dinner the police flicked him and they began a high speed chase. Trina was terrified she asked him "Why won't you pull over?" He said, "This is a stolen car." Trina furthered her story she said, "He was running lights and hitting corners." She said, "It was as though life as she knew it was over."

  She said, "I quickly realized that this was not his first time he definitely had experience she said, "He hit the lights and pulled in someone's drive way pulled all the way to the back and sat there for a minute" That's when I called for a ride and told them where to meet me when they arrived I got out and left. Trina made up her mind never to speak with him again later on, someone asked her. "Did she even think to ask was it his car?" She said, "No because he had the keys." Hey, if the cars are carjacked they will have the keys! Before getting into a car you need to ask is this car yours? You also need to ask to see a license and registration. Don't be afraid to question like have you been drinking or have you taken any E pills. (AKA ecstasy is a very powerful drug).

Whatever state you are in the E pill will heighten it. If you ask him he may not tell you this is why it is good to get to know people so you can study there behavioral patterns. Please know with whom you are getting in the car with if you sense he has been drinking please, do not get in with him. He will tell you he can handle it; but beware and please be wise. There are many young women that ended up in the hospital, jail, paralyzed and dead. Here is something else to pay attention to sometimes we hook up with people that maintain by doing illegal things. If you have children this can be terrible if you have a boyfriend who is dealing drugs and he decides since you're his girlfriend. He wants you to be the one to store his drugs; don't do it. This is a No- no do not hold their guns or drugs for them.

Let me tell you why if the police are watching him and they feel like, they have a cause to obtain a search warrant. Because it's your place, they will say this is your charge. It's your gun your drugs.* If he is not willing to come forward. (They will not check to see whose fingerprints are on the gun). Even if he is there, it is very possible that you still could be held responsible. You could end up with a felony charge. Therefore, there will be no need of crying. Listen the police will say you knew what situation you were getting yourself in. Your boyfriend will say "You knew what I was about when you hooked up with me!" He will then ask are you going to act scary or, are you going to be my ride or die chick? He needs you to take the rap which means we are going to ride it out and if you snitch you are going to die! Please believe it! There are some out there that will kill you; I do not care how much they say they love you. They love their **freedom more**! Now if it is your mom or dads house your parents could end up taking the rap.

This will not be a good thing. I've heard males tell females you do not have to worry if something jumps off I will take full responsibility. Don't believe them! Remember in the early part of the story I spoke of guys dating girls for a long time. The girls did not know their real names. **We have to think ladies.** Please by all means don't be so, in love that if something happens. He can convince you into taking the rap by using lines like "Baby this will be your first offense I already have a record. Listen they will just give you probation or a light sentence." Women either way you will just create an unnecessary record and time away from your; children, family and friends.

If he really loved you he wouldn't have any of that around you any way. You should never have to suffer consequences, which have nothing to do with you that would cause calamity in your world. Be wise! If you believe what they are saying, you are crazy! Before they can get you handcuff his new girl is already there throwing your clothes out and moving hers in so, by the time you make the first call they will have money on your account to receive the call. Afterwards do not expect to much more! If you get pronounced, to a serious sentence the new girl will make her presence known. Your replacement probably will be the one to take your call to inform you, not to call anymore and not to worry. She will be the woman playing mommy to your children. If these are not her intentions she will let you know she doesn't want to play mommy and that your children have been shipped to your parents or she has had them placed with protective services. Don't take my word go visit a woman's prison and listen to some of their stories.

Chapter 15

Do You Know Who You Are?

Karen now wonders will Tim ever know the true qualities. Which she possessed or what he truly had in her. Yes, Karen wanted him to stop drinking, smoking and come to church with her yes; she wanted his soul saved For real. Yes, she wanted Tim to be her partner for life. Karen saw something in him that average woman probably could not see. Karen saw a loving man of God that hid behind a lot of pain which he tried to pacify with alcohol from pass hurts. Although, Tim knew something was missing in his life. He just didn't know what it was that he was missing. Tim was a man that has been shot and bitterly betrayed. He really couldn't find it, in his heart to trust anyone.

Because Tim has not come to the reality, of whom he is! (He is stuck) Yes, he knows what his mother named him. He knows what people, have called him all his life. Question, does Tim really know his identity? Could he really know that God has given him a destiny and a purpose? Does Tim really know to whom he belongs? Does he really know who God is truly calling him to be? Because of the betrayal this man has endured, Tim could not believe that something so real was standing in front of him? On the inside of this Great man was GREAT potential. When others saw him they saw a very dangerous man. However, if they had taken time to get to know him they would have seen a man that would think everyone thinks of me as this strong person. Don't they know I am a human just like them made out of flesh and blood?

He would say Hello!!! Sometimes I need a listening ear. I always do not have the answer? I need someone to talk to sometimes. Whom can I call on? I am bleeding on the inside. Help! Can anybody feel my pain? Cannot they see I have been physically and emotionally wounded? Am I invisible or what? How come they don't see me? Still Tim will get up every day and continues to put his mask on as if everything is ok. Tim is clearly misunderstood he has been through so much but he always manages to make it through, little did Tim know it was the call on his life it was Grace and Mercy that had been covering him.

  The word of God declares when you hear my voice harden not your heart. Choose on this day whom you will serve. Will you continue to let the devil have control or completely submit your will unto God? Here is a man that has done so much in his life, that he could not conceive that God could ever want to use him in; the arena of the pulpit. I must say I beg to differ. Tim was the man that God was calling for; the bible says many are called but few are chosen and he is definitely chosen.

Matthew 22:14   For many are called, but **few** are **chosen**.

That is probably why her connection to Tim was so strong. Besides the streets did not love him "Nor" were kind to him. Karen did she truly cared for him you see she could see far beyond and above; his outer appearance. She even heard his cries in the spirit for help. However, Karen would always let him know I got you baby and she meant it!

Chapter 16

What's the Catch?

So how could Tim not be able to see? He is affecting Karen. It is simple because the world has trained him to think that it is just in a man's nature to have more than one! Whether being man or woman at the end of the day we want to be loved for, who we are and what's on the inside of us. I have found that men who run through women discard them like they are trash usually are impacted by deep trust issues. They are men who have watched their mothers loosely sleep around with different men. It appears they also have been through some type of abuse, physically or mentally not to mention there may have been some form of molestation. Trust me something traumatizing happened. Most times when something traumatizing happens it's locked away and it doesn't surface until something triggers it.

For, instance they grew up feeling like they were pushed to the side or they felt they were the black sheep. Sad to say these things can cause them to grow up becoming caught up in some form of addiction, like alcohol, sex, drugs. Now this does not have to apply to every case. However, it's something to think about as I mentioned earlier, always take notice how a man treats his mom. This is how he is going to treat you! I found that if a man grew up without affection from his mother, if she never took time and nurtured him. He would grow up desperately trying to earn her love and affections. If he somehow he fails at his attempts. He will become bitter, vengeful and disrespectful; towards women. Because a male's mother is the first female that is, suppose to exhibit love to him. If she doesn't when someone exhibits love to him he will not know how to receive it; nor return it back.

He will continually have the thought in the back of his mind. "What's the catch?" This in the end could cost him the love of a lifetime. It is not until he recognizes addresses, then deals with the root cause of his problem. Then he will be able to utilize his findings; to eliminate his demons. Until then it will not be possible to give a woman the love she deserves? He is **bound**, and needs deliverance. What is it that, has him bound **strong holds**- childhood hurt? It could be women, lust, sex, drugs, or alcohol." If I had to take an educated guess I would say the root cause would be Anger/bitterness. A man who is truly ready, who has become in tune with his spiritual side the first time, will tap into her very being (The woman purposed to be his wife). He knows if she's the one although I suggest that he prays to be sure and so, should you, when he finds you he will love you the way you really deserve. You will not have to wonder where he is at night. If you become sick he will be concerned and be there. However, if he hasn't come around yet! You better make sure when you find yourself in devastating situations not to call his number; you **better call** Jesus. Why, because you can bet your bottom dollar he is going to rescue you just in his timing. You can always count on God being there he has no excuses! All excuses have been nailed to the cross. Well this next story was quite a revelation for me. This brother was something else. (Here's how the story went) *** Chris and Tammy were dating Chris was in a car accident and had to be admitted into the hospital. Now Chris told Tammy that she was the only one he was sleeping with but for some strange reason, Chris did not want her there. Ladies check this Scenario out he was in the hospital and almost every hour a different woman came through his door, get this he honestly expected Tammy not to get upset.

One particular woman came in laid her face on his face and kissed him. EVERYONE in the room became silent and looked at Tammy. Tammy immediately got up from her chair let's just say, if looks could kill the young lady would have been dead. Tammy didn't say a word she just sat close to him on his bed with a look on her face like, who is this and why did she just kiss you? Not wanting to cause a scene in the hospital she politely demanded an introduction. Well ladies! When it came to the introduction he said, "Tammy this is Jennifer, Jennifer this is Tammy." Therefore, Tammy continued to question him this made him furious and his response to the situation was, "I have many friends that I knew prior to you." So, Tammy went a little further, she asked well are you intimate friends? Chris replied, "You all are my friends no one is above anybody!" Would you honestly believe he was into her? Answer: No, if he considered her his Godsend he would have made it, known from the beginning not having a problem, with telling the world that she was his girl, not caring who was around. It was at that moment she began to wean herself from him. A few months later she ended it. Tammy truly loved Chris she felt because she accepted his disrespect in the hospital his actions only became worst. ***Troy and Eva met and they said it was love at first sight. Eva was smart and ambitious Troy was quiet and let him tell it, his whole world revolved around Eva. It came to a point if you saw one you saw the other Eva loved him with everything in her. Eva decided that they should go to the next level she got a job and they moved in together. Some months later she became pregnant with their daughter. Going to work and coming home cleaning became her everyday routine; soon it began to take a toll on her. Eva told Troy, "Listen you need to help out and get a job."

Troy wasn't interested in getting a job he felt she had been caring the weight this long why should they change things? The arguments began! Troy began to stay out all night and accusing Eva of cheating on him. He started breaking in her phone. He even disabled her car so, she couldn't go anywhere. It was at this point the relationship turned toxic. Toxic means Poisonous deadly. One evening one of her family members called her saying, "Come and go with me." Eva said, "Okay" Eva didn't think anything of it she gathered her things and went. Eva couldn't believe she ended up over a young ladies house; Troy had been sleeping with, Eva became so angry she broke out all of Todd's car windows.

It was a big altercation Todd knew he had messed up, he began crying and begging her not to leave him. He even threatened to commit suicide, after this event something happened! Troy became far more Jealous and paranoid. He began rigging her phone and setting upset up cameras in the house. Eva became weary she said, "I am tired of paying all the bills." Eva said she felt she was being treated like a prisoner." It was at this point that she decided enough was enough. She left him and began seeing someone else. Troy found out and almost lost his mind. He would say,
 "Eva I can't live without my family. She said, "He would come over my father's house with flowers and candy." She said "Before he cheated she never received anything from him." She said, "Todd would stand outside the house and scream. "I never touched that girl I haven't been with anyone else since we have been dating. Todd became desperate. He went and got a job and he quickly lost the job because he was busy trying to watch her. Todd couldn't eat or sleep. He couldn't focus!

Well he finally wore Eva down and she eventually took him back. Todd's begging had paid off. Eva let Todd know that it wasn't an option; he had to get a job and help out with responsibility. By this point in the relationship Eva had fell out of love with Todd. All the fighting and accusations had caused considerable damage; to their relationship. But, she hung on in there for their daughter. Eva kept saying, "It's something in the back of my mind that won't allow me to give my whole heart back to Todd." One night a guy sent Eva a picture of his private area Eva said, "It was an unwanted picture." Once again Todd broke in her Phone while she was a sleep and became out raged. Eva said, "I was awakened to his hands around my neck and we began to tussle."

She said, "That's when Todd's anger kicked in he grabbed her phone and smashed it." The next day Todd, Eva, and his cousin were in the car. Todd must have had a flash back because out of nowhere, Todd became very disrespectful to Eva in the presences of their daughter. She told him "If you keep it up, I will take our daughter and leave!" Todd nodded his head as to say cool. His cousin questioned Todd saying, "When do you go for your paternity test?" Eva said, "I almost had a car crash." She said I knew he couldn't be questioning whether this was his daughter or not." She said, Todd politely answered and said "I will find out if the little boy is mine this week?" Eva slammed on the brakes and Screamed!!! "Little boy! Todd! What little boy?" He began to say, "Well there is a little boy out there that could be mine?" She questioned, "How old Todd. He replied, "Three years old." She said, "So you know the phone you called her on I pay the bill the car you drove to see her in I bought.

The money you spent dating her I gave you! Yet, you have been accusing me and fighting me?" She said, "Todd you broke my phone for a picture, she screamed! "Todd, you're going to pay for my phone." His response "Was yeah okay after you pay me for my broken feelings." She questioned, "So, you're tripping about your feelings and a picture? Boy! you have a whole baby? At least I broke up with you before I started seeing someone else." Todd told her, "Listen this is the deal I am going to allow you to come clean and remain one hundred." If you can't then I am cool on you! Ladies when did he come clean??? He then screamed, "Give me the keys to my Lexus." As I spoke on earlier she had the jobs. She was the bread winner. Therefore she had to put all the cars and houses in her name. Todd would always tell Eva to cosign everything. He would say I am working on getting employment, so I can step up and help.

However, deep down on the inside Todd knew these weren't his intentions. Well as a result of him not helping Eva's credit was badly damaged. Time went on an Eva was starting a new job but she didn't have a vehicle. So, Todd finally stepped up and put the car Eva was purchasing in his name. Todd's intentions were all bad he didn't help her get a car to help her. He did it to obtain leverage instead she had the Lexus for over a year and she paid every note. But, Todd yet demanded the keys to his car giving Eva an ultimatum she can stay and start their relationship over or find a new place to live. He said if she left she would have to purchase a new vehicle. Breaking News! Eva packed all her things and went to stay with her father. She said, "I'd rather have a peace of mind than material things!" Back to Karen..

Chapter 17

He was Clueless

Karen has been moved by her flesh, far from her purpose. The pressures in her life were so overwhelming it made it easier for her to fall. This is why we have to line up with the word; or simply be left behind. This made it easy for Tim to enter her life. Tim became a breath of fresh air now Tim does not know Karen's true identity! Tim probably thinks she's not focused nor has any drive or goals. Maybe if Tim had realized the weight of destiny that was on her life, he may have realized the gift that was in his presences. Tim's approach was all wrong he took the time to learn her sexual expectations. What he should have been concerned with was learning what she consisted of who knows how they would have turned out?

This kind of reminds me of a story a man came to the United States to find love but didn't let anyone know his true identity or the riches, he possess. He knew if he had revealed who he was, he would not be sure if the persons love would be true. This is why I believe God hides us from certain things and people. God knows what's best for us, even though we might not understand at the time. Sometimes people enter into our lives with bad motives. Have you ever been in a relationship? That didn't work out? When it ended you felt as though you couldn't make it. However, down the line you saw him, and thought.

"What was I thinking? He was really crazy! I can't believe he killed his wife and kids." Then you think!

"Thank God I escaped that bullet."

Chapter 18

You are Going to Deep

So many people take God for granted people don't seem to take the things of God serious. **But Karen indeed knew who she was as well as whose she was; she just wouldn't dare play with sin and try to operate in the things of God. Besides, she could not get with people that were hypocrites, or let us just say people who played church.**

<u>Revelation</u> 3:16 So then because thou art lukewarm, and neither cold nor hot, I spew thee out of my mouth.

This is why she could not straddle the fence. The scripture states you have a form of Godliness but you deny the power thereof. What that means to me is people believe that there is a God but they limit him to what he can do.

<u>2 Timothy</u>3:5 Having a form of Godliness, but denying the power thereof: from such turn away

People definitely don't understand that God is our Master and Ruler of all that he is not just some name; to call on when you're in trouble. God is not a toy that we can pull out of a toy box at will; he is **not** to be **played** with! God is to be honored reverenced and respected. It is written that we are to follow the commandments. I have found when our flesh is in control it makes it harder to follow the commandments. Why, because our flesh is conditioned to follow the ones that make us feel good. We don't want to follow the ones that don't make us feel good. You see you can't live by half of what the word says you have to live your life according to the word.

On the average when this is pointed out people will say all you are going to deep! You do not have to do all that but you really do and trust me a lot more. It's apparent that we can't live our lives any way we choose. We can't allow our flesh to rule our life. If we want to be pleasing to God we must remember, God doesn't make us do anything God gives us free will. Hmmm just a little something to think about! However, back to the reality of things! **Karen must make a conscious decision to reposition her posture so that she can break her fall. Karen has allowed Tim to take her, so high that if she falls something is bound to get broken. Oh yes this fall is going to hurt."** Karen has to now go back and gather her thoughts in order to reposition herself. Karen believed in their love so much she put it on a pedestal. She must now put herself first yes; we have to love ourselves first.

Karen knew she couldn't stay in this state forever, she knew she had to put a plan in motion as she desperately tried to earn his affections. So, when she did return to her first love (GOD) she would have her mate. She wasn't sure, if he was her soul mate. However she was definitely willing to take a chance with him. Sad to say she was torn between the two. Karen felt that being away from things of God was equivalent to, a fish being out of water. Karen felt deep down in her heart that he was the one. However, if you're not careful the enemy will trick you Karen thought the first time they were together; it was bad timing so when they were allowed a second chance. Karen just knew this was destiny. Crazy Huh?

Now, Karen is wondering how did I get here what was I thinking? Why out of all the men pursuing me. Did I allow him a chance to step into my world? Why didn't I keep the door to my heart shut? She thinks, "Oh Yeah now I remember." Karen's family members told her you cannot continue to be stuck up and blow off all the men. You are not ever going to have a man, if you don't take a chance. In actuality Karen was not stuck up she was just guarding her heart. You see she is warm and kind hearted; people generally try to take advantage of people like her.

Karen had a motto about this Karen said, "I was put here with a sole purpose to be used but, never was it intended for me to be misused." She could even recall times when she felt she saw red flags and wanted to back up but her friends would say "I think that man has your best interest at heart. Don't do that man like that." Karen thought "They're right and kept dating him yet, look what state she found herself in. Ultimately, none of this matters! It's apparent that he wasn't serious. She had to tell herself just deal with the pain and find a way to; heal the wounds and move on. Always follow your first mind never allow anyone to cause you to second guess yourself.

Chapter 19

Out of the Skillet in to the fire

Karen spent countless wasted years' in a Marriage where it appeared she was the only one married. I know it appeared that Karen was stupid. However, she was far from stupid she was just praying and hoping Ron would get it together. Karen spent a lot of time meditating and praying, it was in one of those moments when it clicked. Karen began to realize that she kept dating the same man in a different body. Karen jump out of the skillet in to the fire. Karen has found herself in another a relationship that only consists of her.

You are probably thinking will she ever learn? It's been said for women who have a lot of love to give. It is hard to find a man who can return love; in that same measure most men have a problem with honesty. This is why their love usually does not measure up women are generally focused on settling down. While most men are focused on keeping count, of how many women they have conquered. In the beginning, if we pay attention we will probably achieve a different outcome. We generally know from our first conversation rather the man is a temporary or a permanent. If you pay attention there will be signs that will indicate whether he is a temporary or permanent. As women we have a need to be loved because of this we overlook signs that would give us direction. Then we have times we force relationships. There is an old saying if it don't fit don't force it. Here is the thing when you know you have pasted the temporary stage and you stick around, things tend to go too far someone is bound to be bitter or hurt.

You now have two people with; two different agendas. You have a man who wants to make you, an every now and then quick lay, while you are sitting back planning your wedding. One might ask how women keep falling for the same situations. It's simple it is not the man but it is the same spirit. The spirit keeps reappearing just in different men. It's easy to confuse love with lust; when women are lonely. As a result it causes the woman too repeatedly reroute herself in deadly rotations of weakness. This makes it clear that this is her goliath, and everybody has had or has one. If she operates as David did she will be able to slay and conquer her Goliath and move on.

1 Samuel 17:51 [51]Therefore David ran, and stood upon the Philistine, and took his sword, and drew it out of the sheath thereof, and slew him, and cut off his head therewith. And when the Philistines saw their champion was dead, they fled.

I guess it was instilled in Karen to always put others feelings before hers to ensure that she would never hurt anyone. Karen is a firm believer in whatsoever a man soweth. That shall he also reap so she always tries to show; as well as sew love. {What goes around comes around}.

Galatians 6:7: [7]Be not deceived; God is not mocked: for whatsoever a man soweth that shall he also reap.

Now Tim has begun to send mixed signals to Karen He started off saying, "I don't like being single" to telling Karen "I do not have a woman we are not in a committed relationship, besides, what difference does it make you are the only one whom I've been intimate with. Karen thinks, "WHAT!"

Chapter 20

One Summer Night

One summer night Tim invites Karen over so she gets dolled up and goes as she enters, she realizes that he has prepared dinner. Well they had dinner afterwards; Tim invited her outside for conversation. Karen agreed as they were sitting outside a woman name Kelly pulled up. Kelly sat in her car for a few minutes before she got out and approached them. You know how we do ladies we apply the perfume the makeup, when were about to see our man. At first Karen didn't think anything of it. Tim and Karen continued their conversation. Kelly turned her car off and slammed her truck doors and began to approach them all of a sudden Tim paused smiled and glancing up at Kelly. He said, "Hello you look spiffy." Kelly replied "Thanks." There was never an introduction between; the two women. Karen thinks "Hmmm that is strange!"

Tim then tells Kelly to go in the house, with his brother and have a seat. So, Kelly sat in for a while then she came back out she didn't say anything she just got in her car and left. But ladies she returned! Now the time is about two am. So, Karen is wondering why is she here? So, Karen asked him "Who is she?"Tim quickly responds. "That's Kelly I have known her for years. We played in each other's back yards, we have been hanging out since we have been eight years old she's simply a friend of the family." Something in Karen senses tell her different as Karen sits there she realizes that she has a personal emergency and must go home. However, Karen is well aware of the time Karen notice that Kelly and Tim were drinking.

Not a good combination at that hour Karen went home and came back! We all know women have intuition. The house was pitch black. So Karen went to his bedroom window she said, "I stood there for a minute and just listened. I could hear music playing and faint moans. So I knocked on the window." Tim yelled "Who is it? Karen remained silent, and stood there a few more minutes and knocked again." Tim angry at this point screams, "Who is it?" Karen then went to the front door and knocked. Tim yelled, "Who is it?" By this time, as he was opening the door he asked again, "Who is it?" Karen replied "Karen" She said, "Tim had his robe on with nothing underneath it so, I questioned him. "Why are your lips shining and why are you naked. As I snatched his robe open, I immediately became infuriated." However, she needed to do some quick thinking; you see she realized in order to gain entrance into his house she needed to calm down.

So she said, "Hey baby you said I was always welcome. So here I am, I just want to lay with my man." But under no circumstances would Tim let Karen in. Karen became angry and irate. Needless to say she set it off. Tim told her the next day, no one was there even though Kelly's truck was still parked there when she returned he told Karen, "Kelly left with his brother and his girlfriend he assured her by no means was Kelly in the house." He continued to assure her that they all went to an after hour bar. He told Karen he was tired of dealing with her, his reason was he was tired of being accused. He said, "Karen had a problem it was all in her mind, Karen knew if she had gotten in that night things would have gone a whole lot different.

However, this is all wrong I have seen countless times. Women catch their men with other women take a wild guess what's the first thing they want to do (fight). Yes fight the other woman, nine times out of ten she does not even know you exist or he's telling her the same thing he has been telling you. If you feel like it needs to be addressed. Don't try to fight her or degrade her by calling her out of her name. Trust me he has already degraded the both of you. If she knows you are the wife or the girlfriend this could be a little different. However your beef is not with her, it's with him. Remember she can't have an affair without him. He is making you look bad not her. Please address him; we have to learn we are women first. Stop allowing men to create division between us it just gives them more ammunition and makes it easier for them to cheat. Here is something else.

When a man gets caught cheating he is generally quiet. Why, because, he has to think fast in order to figure out how he can defuse the situation and still be able to hold on to the both of you. He may leave or he might ask one of you to leave depending on who he wants to be with the most. If a physical altercation breaks out after you guys are broke apart. He will say something like you came over here and destroyed my things. You need to leave! Just so he can have the opportunity to get in the one who stayed head and sex her, after he accomplishes his mission and she's back on board. He will return his focus to you asking questions like why did you leave? He will say, "You know I hate her, you knew! I didn't want you to leave I was just mad." He will say anything to get you back in his bed. JUST TO MESS WITH YOUR HEAD. Think about it? It's perfect!

He knows the two of you do not like one another. It works out just right for **him**. Listen! He's telling you he doesn't want her then telling her he doesn't want you. Sometimes, they will even use that phrase "She is crazy I don't know what to do she is stalking me." Here is another one of their strategies. He will call your phone let it ring and hang up delete the call out of his call log. When you notice you have a miss call you will automatically return the call, this makes it perfect. He will then show the phone to her and say see I told you she will not stop calling me. I told her I only wanted you. Here is another one. Please state what you have to say over the phone or in person. Concerning breaks ups; let me tell you why. An individual will save your text not respond to your text. So he/she can take the text and use it in their defense. Like see I told you I don't respond to him/her. But in reality he/she have already called believe it, I have seen men do it. While writing I have spoken to men as well as women. I have heard countless stories and here is one that stood out.

***Mya and Roy

Mya told me she had a male friend named Roy that lived out of town. He said to her one evening "It's time for me to go back home." So you know Mya was ready to have sex. She said, "I was thinking **Oh** yes I am about to get him together." But, he said ,"No I'm too tired and besides. I have a long plane ride." Even though she found his reasoning upsetting she took him to the departure port at the airport, not knowing he had his other woman waiting on him in the arrival terminal! So he had to make it appear that he had just come to town. You see, this is why he couldn't touch Mya he needed to be fresh and rested. This is another great illustration for the expression. ~The overlay for the under play.

Mya sense something wasn't right and drove to the arrival terminal, his face was priceless when he realized Mya was sitting there observing like those Homicide detectives. He was busted! I bet he thought homicide was soon to be on the scene. But hey! We all have dealt with some form of deceit. As women we just have to become wiser when dealing with men.

Here is another good one.

A young lady named Lexi was talking to a guy she was dating. One day while he was out driving he and Sue were discussing their date. When, Lexi over heard him tell someone to pull over he then said to Lexi, "Let me call you back my boy out here. Get this Lexis had prepared a nice dinner and a romantic evening. She said, "He showed up the next morning not showered smelling like infection and a fish fry Lexi said, "I asked him what happened to him." His reply was, "I got drunk and fell asleep over my boy's house." His boy yeah right! I told her, "You can believe him if you want to." She was so crazy about him and as crazy as it sounded, she really wanted to believe him. Again, if we don't learn the lessons; that are taught. We will just have to keep repeating them.

****

One day one of my (extended) sons invited a young woman named Toni to spend the evening with him. I thought she was nice and very attractive. However, he did all the right things.

He made Toni feel like she was the prettiest girl in the world so now in Toni's mind she must have been thinking I have to show him that I can be that girl he's been looking for. Therefore, Toni puts all her cards on the table. How, does she put all her cards on the table? First, she reveals her feelings too soon. Second, Toni makes her self- available to him every time he calls. Never always, be available no matter how bad you want to see him! Finally, Toni gave him a few quick sexual favors. Which he openly spoke about to all his friends! Ladies up until this point; he was feeling her. A few weeks later he had change of heart he was ready for something else. Toni found herself caught up she's calling him asking, "Hey can I just come by and give you a hug." He replies, "No baby it is too late it is too dangerous out here." In reality what he really was saying was he did not want to be bothered. He said he kept her around because, he just might have a need that needed to be fulfilled, that only she could fulfill.

I heard him say things to make her feel like he had genuine concern about her safety then he would get off the phone saying, "Toni is a pest!" Maybe if Toni had not given him everything he would have wanted to give her a chance. He may even have wanted to build a solid relationship poor Toni... One day I happen to walk in on some men talking one had been to the spy shop. He had a deodorant can but, it had a hidden camera in it. He said, "He could hook it up to the other TVs. Often he would have select female's that didn't mind being recorded come over and have sex with them. Now here's the thing while the actual sex act was going on his friends would be in the other rooms watching it live. This was clearly a group of **exhibitionist**. Know with whom you are dealing with!

**** One of my extended sons once told me. He will not ever treat a female nice reason being women do not appreciate men that are kind. Plus women respond better when they are being mistreated. He then furthered his conversation saying, "A female's purpose is to have sex after I'm done she is to be left behind." This brother only views women as mere objects to be abused! His motto is to dog females. He said, "You should talk to them like they're stupid and treat them as if, they're trash" then he said, "I am going to show you." He said, "Watch the nastier I treat them the more they are going to want me." I promise you he called several different females put them on speaker and talk to them horribly. I declare they were begging him to talk to them. Unbelievable!!...

***I was speaking with a young woman named Toray.

She began to speak about a situation that occurred in her relationship. Allow me to share a little bit about Toray she's very beautiful very shapely and educated. Toray is well spoken and possess a great job. Some would consider her as a man's dream. Toray said, "My boyfriend always went to bed about eleven, like clockwork one night at eleven fifty five his other line clicked." She said, "He was like hold on but in my mind I was saying "**Hold on**," "Who is this calling him at this hour?" Oh course he gave her some lame excuse causing her to zero in on him and pay attention. Toray then said, "We got to a point where I knew if I didn't call him he wasn't going to call me." Needless, to say his calls became shorter with her.

Also she knew if he wasn't available for her, he was becoming more available to someone else. It got to a point where they did not talk unless she made the phone call she said, "I stopped calling to see what would happen. Three days later he called saying, "I do not feel like I have a girl friend." Toray replied "Maybe you do not need one." All her senses pointed toward another woman even though he wouldn't admit it. He knew he was in the wrong all along, he was seeing another young lady. However, he wanted to keep both of the ladies. So, after a few days pasted he called; to check her temperature to figure out her state of mind.

He had to keep his fronts up so, he pretended nothing had changed they talked through it and everything went back to normal. However, three weeks later he called and asked,

"Do you think we should Break up?" Now Toray's thinking, "Now where did that come from she said, "I was thinking nothing like that, but oh okay." So, they ended their relationship and he went on and married the other young woman. I am sure at this point Toray felt like this was the worst thing ever! Today as Toray views him in his present situation, she is grateful that he did not choose her. Because, she is currently **not** the one being **BEAT**. Remember to always stay in tune with your senses and to trust God when he removes you out a situation.

*** Amy and Josh.

Amy was very pretty and naïve her and her mom had a terrible relationship. Amy's mom always had different men around while she was growing up. Amy vowed that she would never put her children in an environment like that.

One day Amy was on her way to the store while walking she could hear the music blaring from a mile away. As the sound became close Amy began to look around. This black Bonneville pulls on the side of her. The young man in the car said, "Hi I'm Josh!" Now, Josh was light skin with good hair with a smile that would get you in trouble. Amy's words were he was super sexy. Josh asked Amy where you are headed she replied," To the store." He said can I call you sometime? Amy said, "Yes!" They exchanged numbers and it wasn't long before they were talking on the phone everyday all day Amy was in love. Months later Amy became pregnant so her and Josh moved together. Thing were great in the beginning. Josh and Amy were always together.

One night they were out to eat and Amy's water broke she said, "When they got outside his car would not start so, Josh flagged a cab. She said, "I thought I was going to have the baby in the cab I was screaming Josh was screaming, and the cab was swerving. She said, "I can laugh about it now but it was a close call; but, we made it to the hospital, where I gave birth to "Shawn" a beautiful baby boy." Amy became consumed with being a mother and Josh became obsessed with the streets. However, it wasn't long and Amy was pregnant again. This time she had a girl Gabriel Monae. Amy was on top of the world. In the mean time Josh was being pulled deeper in the streets. Amy began to complain because Josh was gone all the time and the bills were getting way behind. So, Amy made a decision to get a job. As a result of this, Amy and Josh began bumping heads so, they split up.

The children were still quite young Shawn was three and Gabriel was two Amy said, it was hard starting over but, then I met Tone. Tone was dark-skinned she said, "Tone looked like, he lived in a gym." It was Tones body that caught my attention. She said, "Tone was very sweet and considerate." A month later they began dating and she moved Tone in great move so, she thought! Her children adored Tone so, he agreed to stay home and take care of the children. Amy said, "I felt comfortable because he was good with my children." Months later something was different Amy said, "I noticed that every time I would come home my children would cling to me, not wanting anything to do with Tone." She said, 'Every time I would try to undress my son, he would become hysterical."

This alarmed her so she called a company that specialized in running wires and setting up cameras. She said, "I had the cameras link to my phone so, if I was not home, I still could see Amy said, "One night while at work Tone had both of the children in bed." She said, "He had Gabriel lying between his legs and Shawn on his side." Amy said, "I was in disbelief she said Tone was putting his penis in Gabriel's mouth then taking it out and sticking it in Shawn's, rectum she said, "Shawn's, screams were the sound of intense torment she said, "I will never forget the look of agony on my children's faces." **The thing that Amy feared the most had become her reality.**

Amy said, "I immediately ran to my car and called Josh" She said, "I was screaming and hollering. However, the words I spoke sent Josh in a rage. Josh told me to, "Calm down and NOT to call the police." Well these things I mentioned didn't go well and definitely, didn't end well for Tone. He did not make it to jail. A few days later Shawn began to gush blood from his rectum so, Amy rushed him to the hospital where the children were examined and taken; Amy said, "It took me two years to get my children back."

2 Timothy 3:6 They are the kind who worm their way into homes and gain control over gullible women, who are loaded down with sins and are swayed by all kinds of evil desires, ⁷always learning but never able to come to a knowledge of the truth.

Ladies **PLEASE** stop meeting men taking them home and moving them in; you **have** to take **time** to get to know these men. You need to look them up on the offender's websites. Take time, do your homework I mean do a real thorough job investigate. Amy said, "If she could tell anybody anything." She would say, "Never allow men to be around your younger children." "**Protect your children!**"

"**LISTEN,**" once your children innocence's have been tampered with or snatched. You don't get a second chance to get it back, or to do, no do over's, protect your children!!!!!!!!!

Back to Karen...

Remember in the early portion of the story Karen disconnected herself from male prospects that were interested in her so, that she would be able to give Tim her undivided attention. Bad move!

Tim hadn't been true! Tim assured her he would be there to catch her, continually repeating he was all she needed now no one is there to catch her. She feels betrayed and deceived she knows in order to regroup, she needs to immediately quiet her spirit to fast, read her bible, and pray so, that she may be delivered and restored. The spirits that are usually responsible and present are usually self esteem, lust, fear, hurt, and rejection. Deliverance is needed once it has taken place and you become released from all the guilt, shame, and defeat. Start your life over and put your trust in God and wait on whatever he has in store for your life.

I know you are probably wondering what happened to Karen. Well since time has gone on, Karen has gotten back in her rightful place with God. She knows that the divorce did not come; to break her and that this particular goal was set up, to make her the strong woman of God that she is purposed to be. What the devil means for your bad, God will take it and turn it for your good. **There is life after divorce and Karen is happy.** The Moral of this story is never deal with a man when you are in a vulnerable state, stay alert and always keep yourself in a place to make wise sound decisions; regarding your heart. Learn how to trust God. **Never allow a man to cloud your thinking to the point; he can piss in your face and tell you its raining!!!!!!!!!!!!!!!!!!!!!!!!!**

www.ingramcontent.com/pod-product-compliance
Lightning Source LLC
Chambersburg PA
CBHW071954070426
42453CB00008BA/792